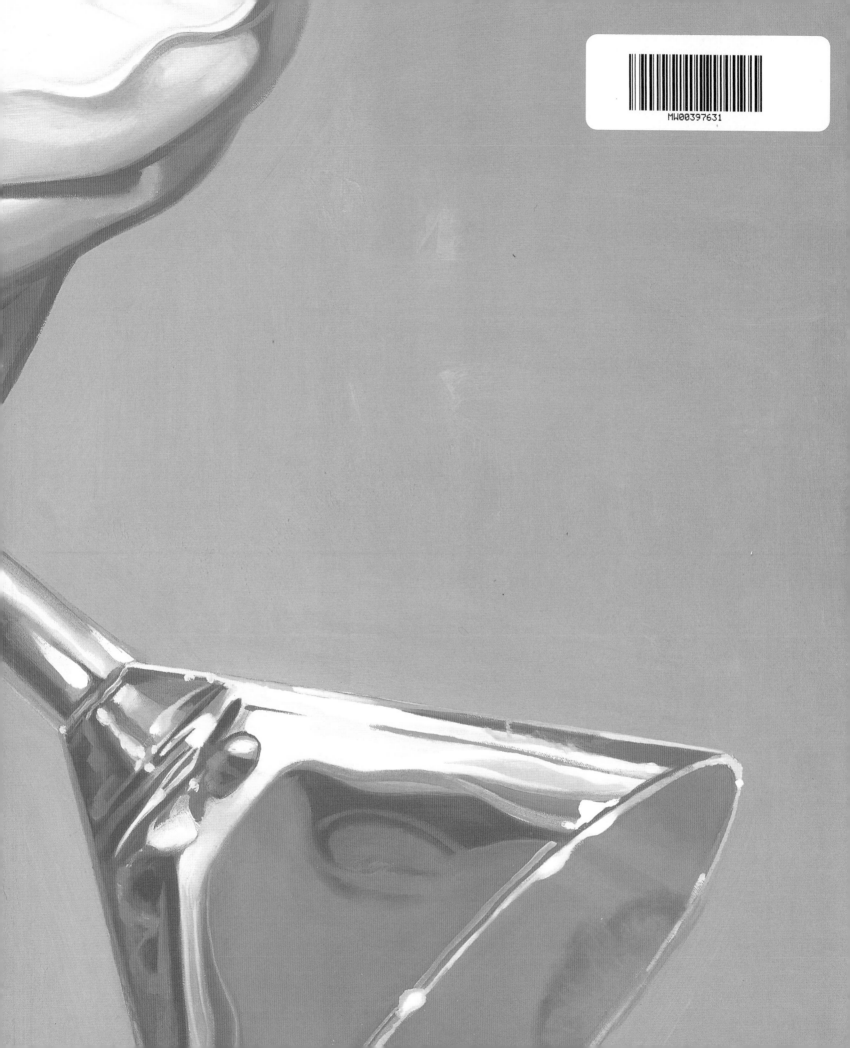

MARK STOCK PAINTINGS

December 6, 2000

For Lori and Ben —
Congratulations — from
your Butler! Mark Stock

MARK STOCK

P A I N T I N G S

For Laurie and Des —

Congratulations and
best wishes in the year
of your marriage —

Barnaby Conrad
2000

BY BARNABY CONRAD III

WITH AN ESSAY BY
MARK HUGH MILLER

DESIGN BY TOM MORGAN

METROPOLITAN BOOKS

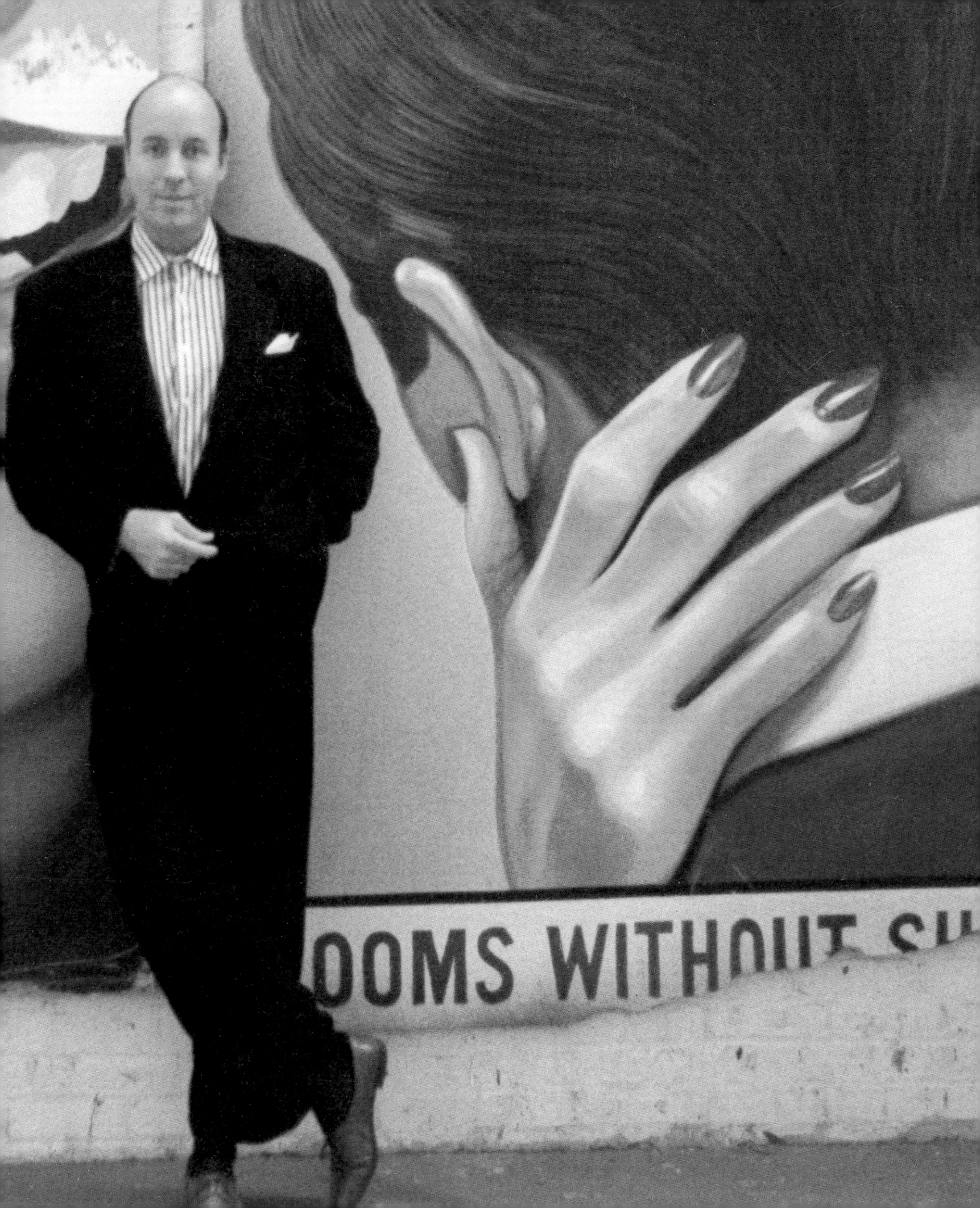
OOMS WITHOUT

CONTENTS

This book is dedicated to the memory of my father Bernard,
mother Doris and brother Ron.

~ Mark Stock

Designed by Tom Morgan, Blue Design (www.bluedes.com).

Printed and bound by Butler & Tanner Ltd.,
Somerset, England.

ISBN: 0-942627-64-4

Library of Congress Catalog Number: 00-105351

The excerpt from *The Remains of the Day* that appears in this book is Copyright
© 1989 by Kazuo Ishiguro. It is reprinted by permission of Alfred A. Knopf,
a division of Random House Inc.

Distributed in the United States and Canada by
Andrews McMeel Universal, Kansas City, Missouri.

Metropolitan Books
a division of
Woodford Press
5900 Hollis Street, Suite K
Emeryville, California 94608

www.woodfordpub.com

PAGE 2: *THE BUTLER'S IN LOVE #25*, 1986. OIL ON CANVAS. 56 X 48 INCHES.
COLLECTION OF JEFFREY AND VALERIE PECK.

PAGES 4-5: MARK STOCK IN HIS LOS ANGELES STUDIO WITH SET PANELS HE
CREATED FOR "SO NICE," STAGED BY THE LOS ANGELES CHAMBER BALLET
IN 1990. PHOTO: ANNE TRELEASE.

PAGE 6: *HOMAGE TO GEORGES DE LA TOUR #2*, 2000. OIL ON CANVAS. 52 X 50
INCHES. COLLECTION OF CHUCK AND BECKY DAGGS.

THIS PAGE: *TICK*, 1999. OIL ON CANVAS. 52 X 62 INCHES. COURTESY OF
MODERNISM GALLERY.

PAGES 10-11: DETAIL FROM *MALE*, 1999. OIL ON CANVAS. 44 X 58 INCHES.
COURTESY OF MODERNISM GALLERY.

INTRODUCTION

"Romantic art means modern art, and that means inwardness, spirituality, color, aspiration toward the infinite, expressed by all the resources art has to offer."
— CHARLES BAUDELAIRE, 1846

Mark Stock has an eye for life's telling moments. Richly detailed and gorgeously painted, his pictures depict people struggling with unrequited love, pondering the consequences of murder, yielding to suicide, and being blinded by obsession.

Stock is an emotional alchemist. He paints male and female lovers embracing in the corner of a cocktail party, romping satyr-like behind gravestones, and sitting morosely on a picnic blanket as their romance dies in the evening light. A barefooted woman contemplates suicide on the edge of a snowy cliff. A handsome, once-vital golfer in plaid pants lies dead in the bosky rough near a fairway, leaving one to wonder: was it a hooked ball to the temple, a coronary over a failing stock market, or an overdose of irony? The paintings veer from Pinteresque darkness to the television glow of soap opera.

OPPOSITE: *THE VIEWER*, 1991. OIL ON CANVAS. 60 X 47 INCHES. COLLECTION OF ADRIANNA POPE.

ACTOR DALE HOWARD, ONE OF STOCK'S CLOSE FRIENDS, POSED FOR THIS PAINTING.

ABOVE: *THE BUTLER'S IN LOVE #33*, 1987. PASTEL ON PAPER. 29 X 21 1/2 INCHES. PRIVATE COLLECTION.

Some of these painted illusions even quote from Stock's personal narrative. His best-known series, "The Butler's in Love," includes several self-portraits that show Stock as a butler who is tormented by his love for the woman who employs him. Social strictures prevent her from returning this love. In fact, she is unlikely to even notice her servant's ardor, for his professional bearing masks his feelings. Although Stock himself never worked as a butler, he says he relates strongly to the butler's social isolation and to the anguish that accompanies unfulfilled romantic obsession. Stock has produced more than one hundred butler paintings, some lustful, some maudlin, some melodramatic.

Stock also twists the tradition of the mercurial harlequin, a centuries-old theme of the commedia dell'arte, when he presents a malevolent clown staring through parted curtains at an object of desire. Then there is Stock's exiled voyeur in a white dinner jacket who gazes intently through a window at the bright lights of society. In the painting *Dead Social Lion*, 1986, we find an outstretched dandy in a white silk suit expiring next to a bouquet of undelivered flowers, as if an impressionist artist had done a painting for a fashion magazine. Out of his turpentine-scented struggles with oil colors and canvas, Stock has created a world where every character knows what tempts him or her and what hurts the most.

Dead Social Lion, 1986. Oil on canvas. 42 x 72 inches.

Collection of Jerry Bruckheimer and Linda Balahoutis.

Opposite: *Disenchantment*, 1988. Oil on canvas. 75 x 56 inches. Collection of Paul and

Cindy Levy. This is one of Stock's first paintings in his "Abyss" series.

DEAD GOLFER, 1988. OIL ON CANVAS. 43 1/2 X 75 INCHES.

COLLECTION OF GAREN AND SHARALYN STAGLIN.

These paintings of lovelorn butlers and star-crossed partygoers invite us into a luminously seductive domain, more like a dream of a cocktail party in a great household than the real thing. The people in this world are dressed elegantly, but their clothes belie their real station in life. Orchestral musicians and butlers may get their clothes tailored at the same place as their symphony's chief benefactor or the tycoon they serve, but, as art critic Kristine McKenna noted in the *Los Angeles Times* (1989), they are, by profession, "powerless players in the world they inhabit. The sense of powerlessness and emotional repression that informs Stock's work is certainly postmodern."

What do the paintings mean to the artist and what do they mean to us? While many bear the emotive power of social icons, they offer no absolutes for interpretation. "I can tell you where the pictures come from," says the artist from his studio in Oakland. "They're scenes from my life. But it's up to the viewer to decide where the narrative is going, to finish the paintings with his own emotions."

Six feet tall, balding, Stock is a born raconteur who delivers his life's details in theatrical strokes. When he speaks his large, quick hands move with dexterity appropriate for a man who is also known as a set designer, jazz drummer, guitarist, magician, and golfer with an enviable four handicap. For Stock, art, theater, magic, and his emotional life mix constantly. "My art and my life intertwine," he says. "There is light and darkness in both. My paintings are mainly about sex and death."

Darkness and light, loneliness and lost love, painful life and painless death. Stock's paintings are both sentimental and ironic, depending on the viewer's in-

clination. While the influences on Stock's art stem more from personal experience than art history, there are traces of past masters in his work. For example,
Dead Golfer, 1988, and *Dead Social Lion*, 1986, were clearly inspired by Édouard
Manet's 1864 painting *Dead Toreador*, but were they homage or spoof? "*Dead
Golfer* has an absurdity to it, I suppose, that could be mistaken for parody," says
the artist. "It's not meant to be. In my pictures I want to call people away from
the ordinary aspects of life — away from the mundane. I emphasize the dramatic moments. Death just happens to be one of those moments."

In many of his paintings of figures in interiors, one senses Stock's admiration
for Manet and Edgar Degas. The off-center composition in Degas' painting
Portraits d'amis sur scène, 1879, resonates in Stock's *The Trumpet*, 1994. In the picture
The Creator, 1989 (opposite page), Stock depicts himself listening to a violinist.

THE CREATOR, 1989. OIL ON CANVAS. 48 X 38 INCHES. COLLECTION OF THE ARTIST.

The work was directly inspired by Degas' *Lorenzo Pagans et Auguste De Gas*, 1871-72, which shows Degas' father listening to a guitarist. The clown and ballerina embracing in *The Kiss #2*, 1992, relate to any number of Degas' backstage scenes of ballerinas. Like Degas, Stock is intrigued by the lighting effects of theater, an outgrowth of his experiences as a set designer. And also like Degas, Stock often works from photographs. Stock is neither as painterly as Manet nor as coolly aloof as Degas. With their open displays of weakness and longing, Stock's paintings play to the crowd. The artist readily acknowledges that the films of Charlie Chaplin were primary inspirations for his paintings of butlers.

And what of his "postmodernism"? Unlike Mark Tansey, another late-twentieth-century painter (see page 14), Stock doesn't paint wry collisions of art history and modern art theory. The fact that Stock has painted himself a dozen times as the butler should tell us something: the art and the artist are not far apart. Two centuries ago, at the beginning of the Romantic period, Johann Wolfgang von Goethe wrote *The Sorrows of Young Werther* (1774) while on the verge of committing suicide over his unrequited love for Charlotte Buff. The writing

ABOVE: MARK STOCK WALKING THE BALL, 1987. PHOTO: BRIAN FORREST.

OPPOSITE: STOCK FLOATING THE DEAD PRESIDENT, 1993. PHOTO: MARK JONES.

ABOVE: *LISTLESS HARLEQUIN*, 1997. OIL ON CANVAS. 74 1/2 X 60 INCHES.

COLLECTION OF TERRY AND CAROL MORITZ.

OPPOSITE: MARK STOCK IN HIS LOS ANGELES STUDIO. 1988. PHOTO: BRIAN FORREST.

ABOVE: *UNDERHANDED*, 1999. OIL ON CANVAS. 54 X 42 INCHES.

COLLECTION OF TIM AND CANDYCE JOHNSON.

OPPOSITE: *THE BUTLER'S IN LOVE—MINUTE SIGNIFICANCE*, 1995. OIL ON LINEN. 60 1/4 X 48 1/4

INCHES. COLLECTION OF RICHARD AND MARY ELLEN SMITH.

helped Goethe regain stability and gave him instant celebrity, although his romantic record encouraged a morbid sensibility among the public. And so it goes with Stock, who seems to have a similar ambition — to emblematize the soul's convulsions.

As a romantic symbolist, Stock wears his heart on his sleeve. He's an aesthete who uses himself in the role of the butler to portray the lovesick man suffering in a cruel universe. His existentialist dandies and self-absorbed lovers seem to exist apart from popular culture. Yet Stock isn't retro and doesn't rely on nostalgia. As Picasso once wrote, "Painting isn't an aesthetic operation; it's a form of magic designed as a mediator between this strange hostile world and us, a way of seizing the power by giving form to our terrors as well as our desires."

Stock's position in the early part of the twenty-first century might be similar to that of Balthus (Stanislas Klossowski de Rola), who painted in Paris in the

1930s, when cubism and other modernist movements were the rage. Balthus kept his distance, expressing his personal obsessions in a style that harked back to the Renaissance. Both Balthus and Stock have created highly personal worlds that remain free of the constraints of time and, therefore, are always relevant.

DETAIL FROM *THE TRYST*, 1988. OIL ON CANVAS. 50 X 63 INCHES. COLLECTION OF BRENDA WOODARD.

OPPOSITE: *THE BUTLER'S IN LOVE #67*, 1995. OIL ON CANVAS. 64 X 50 1/2 INCHES. PRIVATE COLLECTION.

ABOVE: BALTHUS, *LES BEAUX JOURS*, 1944-49. OIL ON CANVAS. HIRSHHORN MUSEUM AND SCULPTURE GARDEN, SMITHSONIAN INSTITUTION, WASHINGTON D.C.

FOLLOWING PAGES: STOCK PAINTING THE BACKDROP FOR "SLEEPWALK," PRESENTED IN 1992 BY LOS ANGELES CHAMBER BALLET. PHOTO: JOE SACCO.

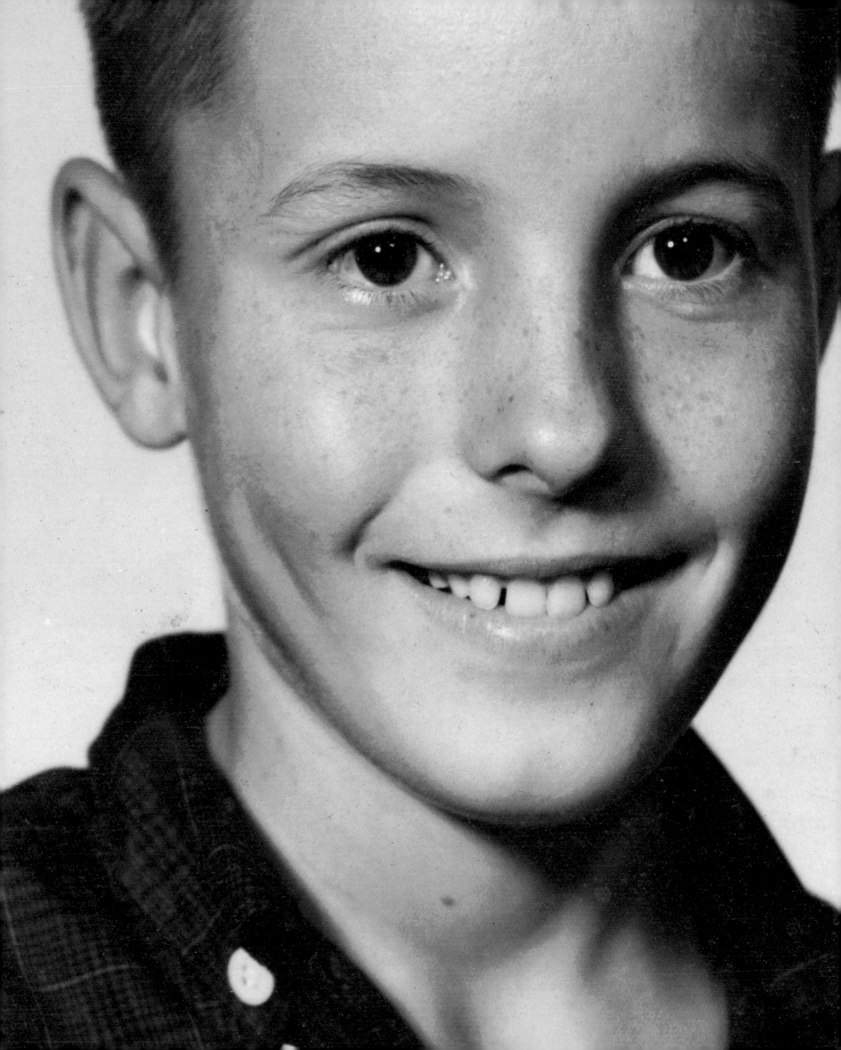

EARLY LIFE

"Painting is only a bridge linking the painter's mind with that of the viewer."
— EUGENE DELACROIX, *JOURNAL* (1893-1895)

One cold windy day when he was eight, Mark Stock stole a tombstone from a Confederate cemetery in San Antonio, Texas, hoisted it into his little red wagon, and hauled it home. He rang the doorbell of his house and presented the trophy to his mother. She wasn't happy with the performance, and Stock's grave-robbing days were over. Years later a friend told him, "You don't realize that stealing that tombstone was your first piece of performance art. That's probably the day you became an artist."

Mark Stock was born in 1951 in Frankfurt, Germany, where his father was serving in the U.S. Army. From a middle class family in Gettysburg, Pennsylvania, Bernard Andrew Stock had married Doris Miers at the beginning of World War II before going overseas. Bernard Stock did not attend college but enlisted in the Army, from which he would eventually retire with the rank of major. Germany after the war was in a state of chaos and ruin, but the Stock boys saw

ABOVE: *PLAYGROUND*, 1979. OIL ON CANVAS. 28 X 28 INCHES. COLLECTION OF DON HENLEY.

OPPOSITE: MARK STOCK AT AGE 11.

little of this from the Army compound at Frankfurt.

Returning to the United States two years later, Mark and his three older brothers grew up as Army brats at several military bases, including Camp Pickett, in Blackstone, Virginia, and Fort Sam Houston, in San Antonio, Texas. Mark failed first grade in Montgomery, Alabama, but his teacher, Mildred Dean, was so sensitive to his early talent that she wrote on his report card, "Keep him encouraged and concentrate on his art. Some day he can make his living with it — I bet!" Instead of commanding him to repeat first grade, Dean presented it as an invitation: "Mark, wouldn't you like to help me with the artwork for another year?" (Thirty years later, Stock located her in a retirement home and thanked her for the early encouragement.)

THE STOCK FAMILY IN FORT SAM HOUSTON, TEXAS, IN AUGUST 1956.

Music and art found expression often in the Stock household. Mark's mother was musical, and his brother Tom (a retired lineman for Florida Power) taught his siblings to play the guitar and drums and also shared Mark's love of drawing. As teenagers, brother Don, Tom, and Mark had a rock band called The Kidnappers. Brother Ron, at the age of ten, hand-set type on a toy press to publish *The Flash*, a two-page newspaper for the neighborhood kids. (Ron went on to become a prize-winning journalist.) "Our mother not only tolerated our activities, she encouraged them," Stock recalled. "We were Army brats, moving from base to base, and had to entertain ourselves. We played war with plastic guns — Germans versus GIs. Sometimes when the rock music or the pranks with firecrackers got out of hand, the neighbors would shake their heads

OPPOSITE, CENTER IMAGE: BERNARD AND DORIS STOCK ON THEIR WEDDING DAY, FEBRUARY 17, 1943.

32

and say, 'There go the Stock brothers again.'"

The somewhat morbid streak in Stock's paintings has its origin in his heritage and home life. One branch of Stock's family was from the small town of Troy, Alabama. His great-great-grandmother was axe-murdered in 1899. The culprits — three men — were caught and hanged. Stock's paternal grandfather shot himself in the head with a rifle when Mark was sixteen. His mother's father shot himself in the head in 1982. Then an aunt on the Stock side took an

e Democrat   Saturday, August 21, 1965

Summer On Playgrounds

DRUMMER WINNER — Winning first place award in the Talent Show at recent end-of-summer Play Day is drummer Mark Stock of Caroline Brevard Park. Competition in tumbling, box hockey, and other indoor sports also featured the Play Day, at Lafayette Community Center. The event was a climax of summer activities for children sponsored by the City Recreation Department.

overdose of pills, tied weights to her shoulders, and hung herself in a coat closet. Stock's own father was an alcoholic who tried to commit suicide with pills; later he was committed to a sanitarium and died shortly thereafter, in 1988. Stock's mother died of emphysema in 1990, and his brother Ron was killed in a car accident in 1994.

"I've got a strange family," Stock admitted. "If some day I get a call saying one of my brothers has been found hanging from a tree I wouldn't be surprised. I'll just say, 'Okay, I'll be there for the funeral.' That's my family. My parents are dead, my two living brothers, Don and Tom, are in Florida, and I'm out here in California making art. But without all that stuff in my life, I might have ended up working as a bank teller. Or maybe as a golf pro."

MARK STOCK PLAYING DRUMS AT A TALENT SHOW IN TALLAHASSEE, FLORIDA, AUGUST 1965.

Being a poor reader, Stock had problems in school and remained in the lower-track classes, but he excelled in sports and music. He developed into a proficient athlete while attending Seminole High School in St. Petersburg, Florida. He became a rock musician. In his senior year, he was elected King of the Prom. He became even better known when, at age seventeen, he tied teenage golf star Buddy Alexander in a citywide tournament. "Buddy was from the country-club set and I just learned by hitting buckets of balls on the public course." (Sev-

MARK STOCK — ELVIS IMPERSONATOR, 1978.

PHOTO: TONY ZEPEDA.

35

eral years later Alexander won the U.S. Amateur Championship.) Stock was so talented as a golfer that many encouraged him to play professionally, but art and music drew him away from the links.

In 1970 Stock entered St. Petersburg Junior College where an influential art professor, James Hagenbuckle, introduced him to the works of Dutch graphic artist M.C. Escher, famous for creating visual riddles. One day, under Hagenbuckle's instruction, Stock drew a disturbing picture of a plant growing into a monstrous giant hand reaching out to snatch a young boy. "Being interested in Escher's work at the time, and marveling at his litho of the hand drawing a hand, I set out to try

drawing my own hand," Stock says, referring to Escher's 1948 lithograph *Drawing Hands*. "Then I came up with the plant scenario. The hand metamorphoses from a plant just after being watered by a child. I felt it was a strong, nightmarish image."

Upon graduation, Stock spent two years on the road as a rock drummer. He traveled all over the South, playing at club after club, living in cheap hotels. He had access to all of the amenities of the rock 'n' roll lifestyle, and there were plenty of women. The name of the band was Crystal Drive, and it played tunes by the Beatles, the Rolling Stones, and Elton John. The group was good, but the rock 'n' roll life wasn't entirely satisfying. Stock decided to pursue the visual arts.

Enrolling at the University of South Florida in 1974, says Stock, saved him from being trapped in a dysfunctional family from a small Southern town. "The university," he adds, "opened my eyes and got me going." A counselor named

Mark Stock watches as Roy Lichtenstein steps in for master printer Serge Lozingot to try his hand
at spinning the ink roller at Gemini G.E.L. Photo © Sidney B. Felsen, Los Angeles, California, 1977.

James Oliver looked at Stock's drawings, announced that the painting classes were filled, and suggested he take lithography. The university had an exceptional printing studio, Graphicstudio, which was funded by subscriptions, sales of prints, and by the state. Famous artists such as Edward Ruscha, Philip Pearlstein, Robert Rauschenberg, and James Rosenquist often came to make prints. Stock studied with Theo Wujick, a master printer who was known at the time for his silverpoint portraits and, later, for large-format pop-influenced paintings that feature scrambled images reassembled into formal configurations. A strict disciplinarian with high standards, Wujcik lead Stock by example. "He was a mentor," Stock says. "He taught me the work ethic of a serious artist. He was a tough critic of his own work. If the work wasn't right, he'd discard it."

Oliver also suggested that Stock take a class on silent film, "The Art of Chaplin," taught by Harry Hurwitz, a filmmaker visiting from New York. Stock hesitated until the counselor added, "No tests. Just watch the movies and enjoy them." As a student who had a hard time reading, this appealed to Stock. Little did he know that Chaplin would become the greatest teacher of all.

"When I saw Chaplin's Little Tramp, I understood him," Stock said one day as he sat in his Oakland studio. "I understood his soul, and that's where my butlers came from. I'm the Tramp! The Tramp's everyone who has been in love and felt pain."

For two years Stock absorbed the techniques

CHARLIE CHAPLIN AND VIRGINIA CHERILL IN *CITY LIGHTS*, RELEASED IN 1931. (BETTMANN/CORBIS)

ABOVE: CHARLIE CHAPLIN AS THE LITTLE TRAMP. (BETTMANN/CORBIS)

OPPOSITE: CHARLIE CHAPLIN IN *THE GOLD RUSH*, 1925.

of printmaking, soaked up the film courses, and became obsessed with Chaplin. After Stock received his Bachelor of Arts degree, Donald Saff, dean of the fine arts department at USF and director of Graphicstudio, recommended Stock for a job as a printer at one of the world's most prestigious print shops, Gemini G.E.L. in Los Angeles. Sidney Felsen, director of Gemini, interviewed Stock over the telephone, and offered him the job.

In the summer of 1976, Mark Stock and a girlfriend, Brenda Woodard, drove from Tampa, Florida, to Los Angeles, arriving at night. They checked into a motel at the corner of Sunset Boulevard and La Brea Avenue, a location Stock knew to be directly across from Charlie Chaplin's old film studio, which had become A&M Records. In the morning, Stock and Woodard walked around the A&M building, pondering the Little Tramp's place in movie-making history. It was a moment mixed with excitement and a bit of nostalgia. Stock then got in his car and found an apartment to rent in the hills below the legendary Hollywood sign. The next morning he showed up for work at Gemini.

The first day on the job he met an Englishman with dyed blond hair who wore one red tennis shoe and one yellow one. "I remember his linen suit," says Stock. "It looked like it hadn't been laundered in weeks and was wrinkled. This beautiful Italian suit speckled with ink and paint! Disheveled hair. He was smoking a cigar. It was David Hockney. I didn't know who he was. I hadn't been exposed to his work before."

Gemini had set up a hydraulic lift so Hockney could angle huge, six-foot-long lithograph stones and draw on them. Known for infusing wit, realism and pop-art inflections into his work, Hockney would sketch from life, then work

DAVID HOCKNEY.
(HULTON-DUETSCH
COLLECTION/CORBIS)

OPPOSITE: ROBERT RAUSCHENBERG, LEFT, AND MARK STOCK COLLABORATING IN 1977 AT GEMINI G.E.L. FOR RAUSCHENBERG'S "ROMANCES" PROJECT. PHOTO © SIDNEY B. FELSEN, LOS ANGELES, CALIFORNIA, 1977.

Great Looking Pine Is a Social Asset, 1979. Pastel on paper. 16 x 13 inches. Collection of the artist.

Varnish Nourishes, 1979. Ink and watercolor. 9 3/4 x 11 1/4 inches. Private collection

from Polaroids as well. As Stock assisted, he watched Hockney draw the famous portrait of Christopher Isherwood, author of *Berlin Stories*, and his lover, artist Don Bachardy. As was customary, the artists sometimes asked for advice from the printers. Hockney would say, "Mark, what does it need — a little something in the background? How about some *touche* in the background?" When Stock pulled a fine, clean proof of the lithograph, Hockney would exclaim, "Lovely!"

Working under the supervision of Serge Lozingot, a master printer who had come to Gemini from Paris, Stock also printed works by Robert Rauschenberg, Ellsworth Kelly, James Rosenquist, Jasper Johns, and Roy Lichtenstein. With their distinctive styles, these artists had little direct influence on Stock's work, yet he felt an affinity for Hockney because he drew portraits and they both

STOCK APPLYING THE ETCH ON A LITHOGRAPHIC STONE. THIS PHOTO, SHOT BY DONALD SAFF, IS INCLUDED IN THE SOURCEBOOK *PRINTMAKING: HISTORY AND PROCESS*, BY DONALD SAFF AND DELI SACILOTTO.

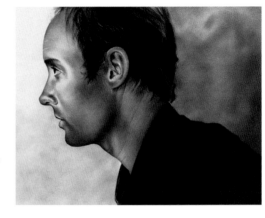

agreed that Chaplin was *the* genius of cinema. "Hockney influenced some of my early prints, but I already had my own style and imagery,"

Stock explains. "What I learned was to respect these great artists — how they worked, how they thought about printmaking, and about art in general. I was really too starstruck to develop a personal relationship with any of them, too shy to carry on a regular conversation. I could hold it together to just print for them all day and then say goodnight." After everyone else left the studio, Stock would work into the late hours, printing his own etchings and lithographs.

"For me, the excitement of working at Gemini was almost equivalent to being a sound engineer on a Beatles album," says Stock. " You felt as if you were part of history, working with these icons of the art world."

After three years at Gemini, Stock left and began to paint on his own. Printmaking itself did affect Stock's early painting. "I painted like a printmaker," he recalls. "That is, I would lay down the background of the painting and let it dry. Then I'd come back and paint in the table, let it dry, put in a vase of flowers and let it dry. Eventually I loosened up and painted wet on wet."

In 1980 Stock got a break. Gene Baro, then curator of prints and drawings at the Brooklyn Museum of Art, invited Stock to show one of his drawings in the museum's soon-to-open exhibition, "American Drawings in Black and White — 1970-80," which included the work of 150 artists. Stock's drawing, a self-portrait, was reproduced in *The New York Times* and praised by chief critic Hilton Kramer, who called it "stunning."

The Brooklyn Museum purchased the work for its permanent collection. Stock also scored a three-year contract with Hirschl & Adler Modern in New York, but the gallery relationship disintegrated. "I was too young," he says. "I wasn't ready for that kind of success and pressure." Car-less and nearly penniless, Stock struggled to make art in his downtown Los Angeles loft, and found work as a set painter for television commercials.

Stock began painting pictures of zeppelins, large foreboding images that have a northern European feeling, perhaps reflecting Stock's years as an infant in Frankfurt, Germany. During a 1985 show in at the Los Angeles Municipal Art Gallery, *Los Angeles Times* critic William Wilson wrote, "They are wonderful icons, loaded with associations — from the elegant decadence of Germany between the wars to the tragedy of the Hindenburg. They bespeak both the weightless silence of futuristic fantasy and the lumpish bulk of dinosaurs. The things are such obvious phallic symbols that they get beyond sexuality and you can't decide if they're ominous or funny."

In Los Angeles, the twenty-eight-year old artist began meeting other painters and dancers. He took an interest in set design and began a decade-long relationship with the Los Angeles Chamber Ballet. While his drawings and lithographs retained an almost Holbein-esque clarity of detail, his paintings took on an expressionist flair. One of his first paintings was of a traditional subject, the artist

SILVERBIRD, 1981. PASTEL AND ACRYLIC-SPLATTER ON PAPER. 7 X 13 INCHES. COLLECTION OF CYNTHIA DRENNON FINE ARTS, SANTA FE, NEW MEXICO.

ABOVE: *DALE*, 1979. LITHOGRAPH. 9 5/8 X 7 1/8 INCHES. PRINTED BY TOBY MICHEL, ANGELES PRESS.

OPPOSITE: MARK STOCK PAINTING *AIRLINER*, 108 X 66 INCHES, IN LOS ANGELES STUDIO, 1982.

PHOTO: IAN COUSINEAU.

ABOVE: *ARTIST AND MODEL*, 1985. OIL ON CANVAS. 66 X 108 INCHES. COURTESY OF MODERNISM GALLERY.

OPPOSITE: *BELLHOP*, 1984. OIL ON CANVAS. 84 X 68 INCHES. COURTESY OF MODERNISM GALLERY.

ABOVE: *SHIP*, 1982. OIL ON CANVAS. 66 X 96 INCHES. COLLECTION OF THE ARTIST.

OPPOSITE TOP: *GERMAN AIRSHIP*, 1982. OIL ON CANVAS. 38 X 46 INCHES. COLLECTION OF BEN AND KATYA KASHKOOLI.

OPPOSITE BOTTOM: *AIRWHALE*, 1982. OIL ON CANVAS. 66 X 96 INCHES. COLLECTION OF PAMELA ROUSSOS AND JIM BENNETT.

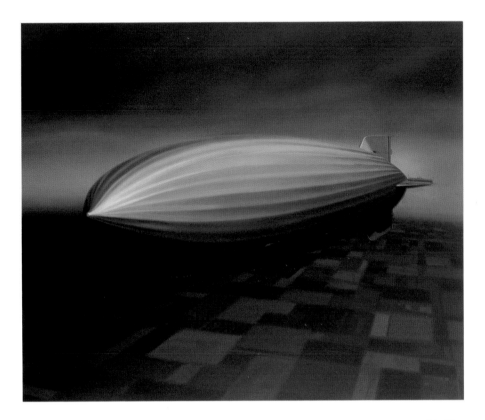

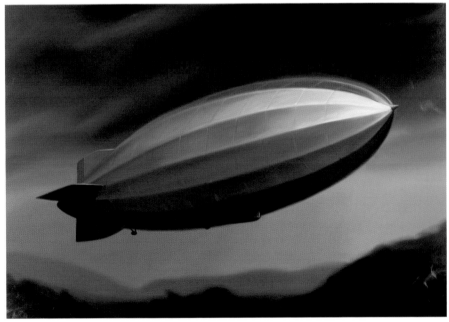

and his model in the studio. The painting is almost monotone, in green and gray with dashes of blue. It was soon followed by a larger-than-life portrait, *Bellhop*, 1984, in which Stock scumbled and swirled brightly colored paint. The painting, Stock acknowledges, took inspiration from Picasso's neoclassical period of the 1920s, and was a precursor of the butler series.

Yet it was film — and a life-changing event — rather than art history that launched the parade of butlers. Chaplin's films influenced Stock immensely. "When I was in turmoil and I painted myself as the butler, I felt like I was making a painting the way Chaplin would make a film," he says. "The butler is the Tramp and the Tramp is the butler, and I'm the butler too. When I finally started painting my feelings through the image of the butler, I felt I had finally connected. It was like therapy for me. Plus, I was honoring my love for Chaplin. I adored the soul of his character, Charlie, with his embarrassment, his jealousy, his shame, his longing. Charlie was a poet and a dreamer. He was lonely, always looking for love. At the end of his life Chaplin said the Tramp was himself. It was all autobiographical. I loved that, and I understand it."

Stock began collecting books about and photographs of Chaplin, and acquired two autographs. Chaplin died on Christmas Day, 1977, a day Stock says he will never forget.

When the distinguished British film critic David Robinson began writing *Chaplin: His Life and Art*, he made a point of interviewing Stock, and wrote this account:

In Hollywood the young painter Mark Stock, who idolized Chaplin and had made a fine series of lithograph portraits, heard the news on the radio early in the morning of Christmas day. Somewhere in

STOCK WAS INFLUENCED BY PRE-RAPHAELITE PAINTERS SUCH AS SIR JOHN EVERETT MILLAIS, WHOSE PAINING *THE PROSCRIBED ROYALIST* INSPIRED STOCK'S *RESPITE*, 1987.

FOREST MURMURS, 1985. OIL ON CANVAS. 75 X 84 INCHES. COLLECTION OF MARTIN MULLER.

ROPE, 1988. OIL ON CANVAS. 36 X 44 INCHES. PRIVATE COLLECTION.

RESPITE, 1987. OIL ON CANVAS. 54 X 64 INCHES. COURTESY OF MODERNISM GALLERY.

the deserted city he found fresh flowers. He drove to the gates of Chaplin's old house and left a rose there. He placed another on the gate of the studio. He found that by climbing up the gate he could draw down the studio flag to half mast; it stayed like that for many days. Finally he went to the Hollywood Cemetery intending to place a rose on Hannah's grave [Hannah was Chaplin's mother]; but a spray of fresh blooms already lay there.

Two years after Chaplin's death, Stock organized a party at his studio and invited several old-timers who had worked with Chaplin. Among them was octogenarian Georgia Hale, who had played the dance-hall girl opposite Charlie in *The Gold Rush* (1925). "She was very quick, with a thoughtful mind," remembers Stock. There was also Charlie's great friend Tim Durant, who had introduced Chaplin to playwright Eugene O'Neill's daughter Oona O'Neill, the fourth and last wife (and mother of actress Geraldine Chaplin). During the evening Stock showed old Chaplin films and the Tramp's cronies reminisced.

"A funny thing happened to me two years later," says Stock. "I had taken Melinda Ring, a dancer and friend of mine, to see a screening of *The Gold Rush* at the Tiffany Theater in L.A. While waiting for the movie to begin, I heard a familiar voice behind me and turned to see Georgia Hale on a date with a younger man. She remembered the Chaplin party and asked how my work was going. The minute her date went out to get popcorn, she whispered to me, 'He doesn't know I'm in the movie. Don't give away my secret.'"

ABOVE: *SUNSET*, 1989. OIL ON CANVAS. 36 X 55 1/2 INCHES. COURTESY OF MODERNISM GALLERY.

OPPOSITE: *THE LOVER*, 1986. OIL ON CANVAS. 57 X 70 1/2 INCHES. COLLECTION OF THE ARTIST.

Los Angeles Times
Friday, December 6, 1985

A moony, slickly groomed young chap in Mark Stock's "Butler."

SANTA MONICA

Mark Stock's work is a young man's art. Populated with smooth-skinned, pretty people, his large canvases and charcoal drawings are overflowing with romantic passion and the conviction that there's nothing more important in the world than to paint.

This belief is no shallow dream, for Stock is a consummate printmaker and draftsman who has an exuberant way with paint and a penchant for dramatic circumstance. Indeed, here is someone for the people who think artists today don't know the first thing about making real art.

Stock takes his talent and runs with it—often to melodramatic ends in a show that charges realism with emotional turbulence. His yellow light turns lurid in an untitled canvas centering on unspoken tension among three men. In that and other works, a secretive, lustful atmosphere is thick enough to cut with a palette knife. Even so, it's thrilling to see how red light plays around the lapel and cuffs of a dark suit or to be swept away by the elegance of fabric covering a lovesick man's back.

The most prevalent character (probably a self-portrait, to some degree) is a moony, slickly groomed young chap in a tuxedo. He seems to be in the throes of a crisis as he bangs his head against a wall, gazes from a balcony or simply leans off-balance against a wall. A wealthy young narcissist who has nothing to do but emote? Well, no. The titles announce, "The Butler's in Love." We should have guessed from the tell-tale white gloves.

Portraying handsome servants in elegant dress (one painting depicts a bellhop in a flaming red suit against a turquoise background) gives the work an intriguing social twist. No persecuted vassals, neither are these characters ordinary working stiffs. Everything about them is so theatrical that we watch them as if they are characters in a play. (Torture Gallery, 2917 Santa Monica Blvd., to Dec. 21.)   —S.M.

BUTLERS AND VOYEURS

"You will often find me appraising a picture exclusively for the sum of the ideas or of dreams that it suggests to my mind."

— CHARLES BAUDELAIRE, 1855

In 1978 Stock's personal life, his fantasies, and his art began mixing and influencing each other in strange ways. A woman who had seen his art at the Brooklyn Museum of Art exhibition called him up in Los Angeles. She began selling Stock's work, and a transcontinental romance grew via telephone.

"I always get these women who are weird," says Stock. "My work seems to attract women who are desperate and passionate. I like the adventure, the suspense. We used to speak for hours on the phone. Finally she had to come out to L.A. I met her at the airport. She'd sent me a snapshot, but I didn't really know what she'd be like. Well, she arrived and she was beautiful.

"I was a little nervous and so was she, but I had a plan," he recalls. It would be the first time Stock influenced real life with the romantic fantasies found in his art.

ABOVE: A REVIEW IN *THE LOS ANGELES TIMES* IN DECEMBER 1985,

FEATURING *THE BUTLER'S IN LOVE #1*, 1995, COLLECTION OF HENRY V. HEUSER JR.

OPPOSITE: *THE BUTLER'S IN LOVE #37*, 1987, 68 X 53 INCHES, COLLECTION OF DAVID LEE.

"I told her, 'Remember those letters I wrote about my solitary walks in the Hollywood Hills near the sign? I'll take you there.'"

They drove and parked as dusk came on. The hillside was thick with weeds and underbrush and they picked their way carefully. "It was a little scary," he recalls, "because the Hillside Strangler was still on the loose, but it was also romantic." As they came around the bend in the trail, they looked up the hill to see a butler standing beside a table illuminated by a ring of candlelight. The Hollywood sign loomed in the background. The woman gasped. She didn't know that Stock had arranged for a friend to pose as the butler. "Oh my god, this is good," Stock thought as he smiled, squeezed the woman's hand and said casually, "Hey, this is nice."

As the couple reached the table, the butler seated them silently, lifted a bottle from a silver ice bucket, and poured champagne. The sun had set and stars lit the sky. The lights of the city glistened. It was half real, half illusion. Standing at a modest distance in the dry underbrush, the butler approached only to refill the champagne glasses. As Stock took her hand, the woman began to cry with astonishment.

After a while Stock said, "Why don't we walk some more?" With the moon rising in the night sky, the moment was overpoweringly ripe. They stepped off the path in Beachwood Canyon and lay down in a grassy clearing. When they eventually walked back, the butler had packed up everything and disappeared. The woman was so stunned by the experience that they drove down the hill to the flatlands in total silence. "It was as if I had put her in a movie of her fanta-

THE BUTLER'S IN LOVE #17, 1986. OIL ON CANVAS. 56 X 48 INCHES.

COLLECTION OF MICHAEL AND BONNIE MOE.

sies," says Stock. "I was pretty taken in by it myself, because the butler played his role so perfectly. I never did that again."

Stock eventually did two paintings, *Rapture I* and *Rapture II*, 1995, that captured the event. The enchanted evening on the hillside also appeared in a scene in *Fleshtone* (1993), a movie inspired by another romance by telephone. "Basically the film script came out of a relationship I had with a woman," says the artist. "She used to call me at all hours. She was an interesting person, well-read, educated, mysterious. Our relationship was weird."

She also knew how to turn on a lonely butler. Stock later described the phone encounters to Harry Hurwitz who, a decade before, had taught the university film course on Charlie Chaplin. Intrigued, Hurwitz expanded Stock's story into a screenplay. *Fleshtone* was shot on a low budget in South Africa and released in 1993.

The movie is about a young artist named Matthew Greco who, coincidentally, paints butlers. Stock's paintings appear throughout. In the beginning of the film, a woman approaches the artist at his gallery opening and asks about the butler paintings. Greco explains: "You see the butler — he's a lonely guy thinking about the woman, the woman he can't have because he's beneath her, unworthy of her. The more unattainable the woman is, the more he wants her. The more he wants her, the more he suffers. The more he suffers the pain of rejection, the more turned on he gets."

The woman gazes at the paintings, then replies somewhat dizzily: "The butlers are sexy. They really turn me on."

The artist-protagonist meets another woman over the phone and paints her nude portrait from a photograph she has sent him. Before they can meet, she ends up

COVER OF THE *FLESHTONE* VIDEO, PUT OUT BY PRISM PICTURES IN LOS ANGELES. PRODUCED IN 1994, THE VIDEO IS LOOSELY BASED ON AN INCIDENT IN MARK STOCK'S LIFE.

murdered. Well, not exactly. Because the woman on the phone and the woman in the picture are not the same person. And our artist hero finds he's been set up as a prime suspect in a murder case. In the end love, sex, death in equal parts made for a "flawed but interesting" soft-core porn-action film that, well, has its moments. Especially the murder (featuring an ice pick through the eardrum) during a flight into the Los Angles air terminal. Though *Fleshtone* "went straight to video," as they say in the business, Stock was pleased with his entrée into film. *Fleshtone* has had repeated showings on HBO and on European television.

Does art copy life or does life copy art? "Neither," says Stock. "They coexist. There's a fine line between the two worlds, and I like walking that line — stepping on one side, then the other. My art also juxtaposes joy and sorrow, which gives you the pathos that Chaplin understood so well."

Two years after the romantic encounter under the Hollywood sign, the twenty-nine-year-old Stock fell in love with Suzy Felsen, daughter of Gemini director Sidney Felsen. Like the art dealer from the East Coast, Suzy, who is ten years younger than Stock, inspired another of his real-life mixes of affection, fantasy and theater. "I wanted to do something romantic for her," he says. "Something as great as the butler on the hillside, something she would treasure. That was it — treasure!"

Stock built a treasure chest out of wood and painted it to look old. Inside he put a bottle of wine, two glasses, a corkscrew, and a blanket. He carried the chest down to the Santa Monica beach and buried it. Pacing off the distance from the

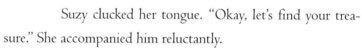

cliffs and the lifeguard station he drew a map on parchment, singed the edges and "weathered" it with tea stains. That evening after dinner, he took Suzy for a walk on the beach. The sun had just set. As they walked, Stock casually dropped the map behind him. "Hey, what's that?" he said absently.

"Probably nothing," Suzy said. "Just paper."

"Oh, yeah?" He picked up the map. "Looks like a map of some kind. An old map. Here's a circle with an X. Maybe it's a treasure map."

"Oh, really?" she said dismissively.

"Yeah, but look," he said, holding the map up in the moonlight. "Here's the Pacific Coast Highway and it says twenty paces to the north from the lifeguard station and . . ."

Suzy clucked her tongue. "Okay, let's find your treasure." She accompanied him reluctantly.

Following the map's instructions, he began to pace off the distances. "Seven steps to the ocean . . . then twelve steps north to the house on the hill and . . . " He stopped. "I think this is the end. We're here. What do I do now?"

"Dig, silly!"

Stock began to scoop sand. Suzy sat down and watched. He dug deeper and deeper, until he hit something hard and hollow. He scrambled backward. "There's something down there!"

Suzy knelt in the sand and peered cautiously into the hole.

"Didn't I tell you this map was important?" shouted Stock.

ABOVE: MARK STOCK IN PETER FOE'S PHOTOGRAPH "MAN FEIGNS CONTEMPLATION,"

TAMPA, FLORIDA, 1992.

OPPOSITE: *THE BUTLER'S IN LOVE*, 1991. OIL ON CANVAS. 20 X 16 INCHES.

COLLECTION OF BARNABY CONRAD III

ABOVE: PHOTO COLLAGE AND STUDY, 1998.

OPPOSITE: *THE BUTLER'S IN LOVE*, 1998. OIL ON CANVAS. 87 X 72 INCHES.

COLLECTION OF PAMELA ROUSSOS AND JIM BENNETT.

THE BUTLER'S IN LOVE #68, 1994. OIL ON CANVAS. 57 1/4 X 46 1/2 INCHES.

COLLECTION OF GUY LAMPARD AND SUZANNE BADENHOOP.

OPPOSITE: *THE BUTLER'S IN LOVE #59*, 1991. OIL ON CANVAS. 96 X 79 1/2 INCHES.

COLLECTION OF THE ARTIST.

"You're always pessimistic! You never believe in this kind of stuff!"

He reached down into the hole and hauled up the treasure chest. "Who knows what this is?" said Stock. "It could be a dead baby, or a person's head. I don't know — maybe we should call the police."

Suzy sat frozen. Mark pried open the box with as much drama as possible. He flipped the lid open. He withdrew an envelope, stared at it in the moonlight, and handed it to Suzy. "Why — it's for you."

"It's for me?"

While she opened the envelope and read the love letter, he pulled other items from the chest — the bottle of wine, a corkscrew, the glasses, the blanket. Suzy's bewilderment turned to appreciation for the magic in the performance. They eventually left the chest on the beach, but she kept a piece of it as a souvenir.

Mark and Suzy were together for a year and a half. Then it ended and they never resumed the relationship. But their eighteen months together would affect Stock's art for the next two decades. "It was a painful breakup for both of us," he acknowledges. "The sadness inspired the butler paintings. In a sense, the memory of Suzy became a muse for me. It allowed me to paint my melancholy." Suzy went on to become a recognized fine-jewelry designer.

Stock stopped painting still lifes and zeppelins, and plunged into the figure on a grand scale. "It was as if I'd finally found a keyhole into my soul," he says. The first of the butler paintings made its debut at the Tortue Gallery in Santa Monica in December 1985. Like most of the paintings in the show, the first

ABOVE LEFT: *THE BUTLER'S IN LOVE #63*, 1994. OIL ON CANVAS. 24 X 18 INCHES.

COLLECTION OF MR. AND MRS. GEORGE E. MCLEOD.

ABOVE RIGHT: *THE BUTLER'S IN LOVE #66*, 1994. OIL ON CANVAS. 64 1/2 X 50 1/2 INCHES.

COLLECTION OF VICKI AND KENT LOGAN.

OPPOSITE: *THE BUTLER'S IN LOVE*, 1999. OIL ON CANVAS. 54 X 42 INCHES.

COLLECTION OF CARLSTEN AND GAIL ANDERSEN.

ABOVE: *THE BUTLER'S IN LOVE — MINUTE SIGNIFICANCE*, 1999. OIL ON CANVAS. 44 X 36 INCHES.

COLLECTION OF MR. AND MRS. DUNCAN A. CHAPMAN.

OPPOSITE: *THE BUTLER'S IN LOVE*, 1987. ETCHING, DRYPOINT AND AQUATINT, ED. 28. 27 1/4 X 22

INCHES. PRINTED BY JAMES F. LORIGAN. COURTESY OF MODERNISM GALLERY.

FROM *THE REMAINS OF THE DAY* BY KAZUO ISHIGURO (1989)

Lesser butlers will abandon their professional beings for the private one at the least provocation. For such persons, being a butler is like playing some pantomime role; a small push, a slight stumble, and the façade will drop off to reveal the actor underneath. The great butlers are great by virtue of their ability to inhabit their professional role and inhabit it to the utmost; they will not be shaken out by external events, however surprising, alarming or vexing. They wear their professionalism as a decent gentleman will wear his suit: he will not let ruffians or circumstance tear it off of him in the public gaze; he will discard it when, and only when, he wills to do so, and this will invariably be when he is entirely alone. It is, as I say, a matter of "dignity."

It is sometimes said that butlers only truly exist in England. Other countries, whatever title is actually used, have only manservants. I tend to believe this is true. Continentals are unable to be butlers because they are as a breed incapable of the emotional restraint which only the English race are capable of. Continentals — and by and large the Celts, as you will no doubt agree — are as a rule unable to control themselves in moments of strong emotion, and are thus unable to maintain a professional demeanour other than in the least challenging of situations.

OPPOSITE: ANTHONY HOPKINS AS THE BUTLER STEVENS IN THE

1993 FILM *THE REMAINS OF THE DAY*. (PHOTOFEST)

butler was loosely painted, and a *Los Angeles Times* critic commented that the canvases were "overflowing with romantic passion and the conviction that there's nothing more important in the world than to paint." The newspaper reproduced *The Butler's in Love #1,* 1985, and noted that "portraying handsome servants in elegant dress . . . gives the work an intriguing social twist. No persecuted vassals, neither are these characters ordinary working stiffs. Everything about them is so theatrical we watch them as if they were characters in a play."

Stock has painted more than a hundred butlers, each one unique. A number are clearly self-portraits, but others are of friends dressed in the butler's livery. These solitary, anachronistic figures seem captured in the middle of emotional chaos. Around the impeccably dressed manservant, the paint flies off in garish, melodramatic splashes that imply ecstasy, pain, or longing. The agitated painterly backgrounds serve as a counterpoint to the butlers' expressions of mental concentration. "I paint people thinking," says Stock, "and I try to capture them in the moment." Just what they are thinking is up to the viewer to decipher.

The butler paintings, he adds, "fill up an inner emptiness" and offer him therapeutic release. "It helps me feel complete to paint this solitary person. I am comfortable with solitude; it has been my teacher, my motivator."

Stock had been painting butlers for five years before the British novelist Kazuo Ishiguro published *The Remains of the Day,* in 1989. The novel is a tragic tale of the ultimate English butler, Stevens, who works at a great English manor, Darlington Hall, in the 1930s. This butler denies himself a life of romantic love and indi-

DAN MCCLEARY, *DOCTOR EXAM-
INING WOMA'NS EAR*, 1982. OIL ON
CANVAS.

viduality not only to serve Lord Darlington but to keep up the ideals of true butlerhood. Once he discovered the book, Stock immediately corresponded with the novelist by letter. The artist was further pleased when Merchant Ivory released the 1993 film based on the novel, with Anthony Hopkins as Stevens, the butler who sacrifices everything for duty.

In one scene, Miss Kenton (played by Emma Thompson), the housekeeper who is in love with him, says, "Ah, but I've noticed it, Mr. Stevens. You do not like pretty girls to be on the staff. Might it be that our Mr. Stevens is flesh and blood after all and cannot fully trust himself?"

Stevens replies, "Really, Miss Kenton. If I thought there was one modicum of sense in what you are saying I might bother to engage with you in this discussion. As it is, I think that I shall simply place my thoughts elsewhere while you chatter away." And yet later Miss Kenton discovers him reading an old-fashioned sentimental love story, which gives her hope, but little more. Stevens has so blocked his heart that he feels only twinges of emotion for the love-struck Miss Kenton.

In contrast with Ishiguro's glacial hero, Stock's butlers are so passionately in love or lust that only with the greatest restraint can they fulfill their duties as a gentleman's manservant. Stock paints them Hamlet-like, at the very moment they wrestle with the dilemma.

In 1983, the painter Nancy Reese knocked on Stock's studio door and introduced him to Dan McCleary. The thirty-one-year-old McCleary was just becoming known for his paintings depicting private glimpses of people in fast-food restaurants and other public spaces. Stock felt a connection to McCleary's painting and, with his new friend's encouragement, began concentrating on a more narrative approach.

OPPOSITE: *THE VIEWER* #3, 1990. OIL ON CANVAS. 74 1/2 X 64 1/2 INCHES.

COLLECTION OF MR. AND MRS. PETER TRETHEWEY.

"Besides sharing painting ideas, Dan and I were also interested in movies," Stock says. A typical evening for the young artists included dinner at the nearest Sizzler steak house and then a movie. Later they would walk through the Hancock Park area, taking in the beautiful homes of early Hollywood.

"We were voyeurs," says Stock. "We peered into the windows of the wealthy and created our own stories of who these people were and what they did in life. Our scenarios would ultimately turn to the morbid as we imagined social mayhem taking place behind those walls."

In the late eighties, Stock began painting a series called "The Viewers." Art writer Kristine McKenna wrote in *Los Angeles Times* in 1986: "Gazing into space and lost in melancholy reverie, these sad dandies are sinking in a quicksand of wealth, star-crossed romance and the anguish of ambitions that go beyond one's birthright." Here the Tramp and butler have been replaced by a dapper figure in summer evening dress — a man in a white tuxedo. It's evening at an elegant home near Los Angeles or Montecito, or perhaps it's Southampton or Palm Beach. Slipping away from the chatter of cocktail conversation, a man in a white dinner jacket walks outside to the garden, then approaches a window and looks in. What does he see — the party he has wandered away from? The woman he loves from afar and is too shy to approach? Or is it a more intimate room of the house, perhaps a bedroom? Is this his first time as a voyeur — or an obsessive pastime? "I've done my share of peaking in windows, sometimes with devastating emotional results," says Stock. The artist also nods, once again, to the influence of Chaplin, particularly the poignant image of Charlie staring in the window of the brightly lighted saloon in *The Gold Rush* (1925).

THE VIEWER #8, 1990. OIL ON CANVAS. 74 1/4 X 64 1/4 INCHES. COURTESY OF MODERNISM GALLERY.

OPPOSITE: CHARLIE CHAPLIN SPOTS GEORGIA IN *THE GOLD RUSH*, 1925, AN INSPIRATION FOR STOCK'S "VIEWERS" SERIES.

ABOVE: *THE VIEWER #14*, 1991. OIL ON CANVAS. 39 1/4 X 37 INCHES.

COLLECTION OF KILE AND JUDY MORGAN.

OPPOSITE: *THE VIEWER #6*, 1990. OIL ON CANVAS. 96 1/2 X 72 1/4 INCHES.

COLLECTION OF VICKI AND KENT LOGAN.

THE STAGE

"Will you, won't you, will you, won't you, will you join the dance?"
—LEWIS CARROLL, *ALICE'S ADVENTURES IN WONDERLAND*, 1865

MARK STOCK'S *BROOM CHAIR*
WAS INSPIRED BY MARCEL
DUCHAMP'S *BICYCLE WHEEL*,
1913. STOCK LATER DEVEL-
OPED THE PIECE INTO A SET
FOR "TRACERS," A MODERN
DANCE PRESENTED IN 1981 AT
UNIVERSITY OF CALIFORNIA
AT LOS ANGELES' ROYCE
HALL BY THE RUDY PEREZ
DANCE ENSEMBLE.

After attending an American Ballet Theater production of "Swan Lake," starring Rudolph Nureyev, Stock immersed himself in dance. He studied modern dance with Karen Goodman and ballet under Sally Gunther. He also began designing sets and costumes for several Los Angeles-based choreographers, including Goodman, Rudy Perez, Stanley Holden, Tina Gerstler, Raiford Rogers and Victoria Koenig.

Stock did seven projects for the Los Angeles Chamber Ballet (LACB), in-cluding the set design for the company's production of Antoine de Saint-Exupéry's *The Little Prince* in 1986. This is the story of the child Prince who crash-lands on a far-off planet, and can only return to Earth after a potentially fatal confronta-tion with the Snake, an allegorical representation of Destiny. A fighter pilot during both world wars and a commercial aviator in South America, Saint-Exupéry wrote the story just a year before he was killed in action in World War II, in

OPPOSITE: WORKING ON THE SET FOR BALLET PACIFICA'S PRODUCTION OF

"PERSONAL STATEMENTS — COMMON KNOWLEDGE," 1992. PHOTO: DONALD FARNSWORTH.

1944. There is a theory that he wrote *The Little Prince* to prepare children and other young people in wartime Europe for the eventuality of death. Stock had a field day with the set and costumes, and a *Variety* review praised his design as one that "adroitly reflected the spirit of Saint-Exupéry's naive, subtly symbolic tale." The article also touted Stock's design of the smoking wrecked airplane as "a tour de force."

Then came "Orpheus," in 1988, an adaptation of Ovid's *Metamorphosis*. Again, it is a story about death. Orpheus descends into Hades to visit his dead wife Eurydice. He convinces the gods to allow her to return with him on the condition that he not look at her until they are out of the underworld. He can't resist, and Eurydice dies again. Stock painted a backdrop inspired by the art deco bridge at Fourth Street in downtown Los Angeles. "I was driving around looking for

BELOW: THE SET OF "THE LITTLE PRINCE," 1986. PHOTO: ERIC YANAGI.

OPPOSITE: MARK STOCK FALLS INTO LINE WITH HIS NEWLY FABRICATED *BROOM CHAIRS*.

Stock's set and costumes for "Orpheus," an adaptation of Ovid's *Metamorphosis*, presented by the Los Angeles Chamber Ballet in 1988. Photo: Eric Yanagi.

something out of the ordinary and the bridge struck me as sinister. I painted it in ultramarine blue, moonlight colors," he says. "The trompe l'oeil effect was so good that after one performance a woman came backstage to ask what I had carved the details out of. I told her, 'It's a painted drop!'"

In 1989, Stock collaborated with the LACB to create the sets for "Dmitri," a ballet based on a comic scenario from Woody Allen's 1975 short-story collection *Without Feathers*. The libretto, from Allen's satirical piece "A Guide to Some of the Lesser Ballets," is a spoof on Fokine's "Petrushka" with a few pokes at "Giselle." That choreographer Stanley Holden was able to squeeze twenty minutes of dance out of a comic synopsis only six paragraphs long is an absurdly pleasant miracle. ("No one in their right mind would want to try it," Allen reportedly commented, but he was swayed to allow the adaptation and performance through the intercession of actress Paula Prentiss.)

The story is simple: a fool named Leonid is so in love with Natasha that each evening he places a giant basket of mixed vegetables and salads on her doorstep to show his devotion. This inspires the "Dance of the Mixed Greens." Natasha likes Leonid but at a carnival show falls in love with a puppet named Dmitri. Leonid tries to kill the puppet, but succeeds only in damaging its arm. The ballet ends with Dmitri and Natasha on the roof of

BELOW: STOCK AND PAINTER JOHN NAVA WORKING ON A BACKDROP FOR THE LOS ANGELES CHAMBER BALLET PRODUCTION OF "ORPHEUS," 1988. PHOTO: ANNE TRELEASE.

the Merchant's Bank, with Natasha plucking the straw stuffing from Dmitri's wounded limb while Leonid tries to commit suicide by drinking Air Wick.

Instead of setting the ballet in a quaint little hut in the vineyards, Stock chose L.A., where he put Natasha in a stucco tract home complete with TV aerial and a coiled green garden hose from Sears. Stock also painted a beautiful futuristic Ferris wheel that actually moved, a fortune-teller's booth that doubled as a first-aid station, and carnival tents. In the background loomed a twisting section of the Ventura freeway. Jan Breslauer wrote in the *LA Weekly* (February 23, 1989): "Like Allen's humor, Stock's images create a surface giddiness with an undercurrent of somber thought. Beyond the gently rounding freeway and the grassy field, something tragic lurks. Happiness is fleeting, hope springs stupidly eternal and lovers never learn. *Heavy sigh.*"

A dancer himself, Stock played three small character parts in the ballet. He remarked later: "There's really nothing quite like dancing across your own set — except watching the performance of someone who can *really* dance."

Stock collaborated with choreographer Raiford Rogers again in 1990 when the

LACB went back to the future for inspiration. "So Nice" was billed as the bossa nova meets Betty Crocker, Brylcreem, and bowling, circa 1957. Rogers said he wanted to be "superficial and interesting at the same time." And, as so many in L.A. do with that recipe, he succeeded.

To evoke the period, Stock painted eight-foot-high billboards of Betty Crocker, fingers caressing

THE "MIXED GREEN SALAD," ONE OF THE PROPS STOCK DESIGNED AND PAINTED FOR THE SET OF

"DMITRI." PHOTO: ERIC YANAGI.

Brylcreemed male hair, Fig Newtons as big as suitcases, and a giant fork poking a sizzling T-bone steak. The music was right out of the summer of 1957 with the bossa nova and the Fleetwoods. Stock painted the sets quickly, then distressed them to give them an aged look. Rogers gave him free rein. "I loved Raiford's aesthetic, and the way I was treated as an artist," says Stock. "They tell me the theme, I come up with the concept."

Painting scenery, Stock observes, is a lot different from producing fine art. "It's looser and a lot bigger, so it 'reads' at a distance. It's more exaggerated. It's actually quite liberating, because I'm not worrying about art history. It's pure technique: easy, and so much fun." The set for LACB production of "Sleepwalk" (1992), which consisted of a giant woman wearing a sleep mask, was inspired by the backdrop of giant locomotive in Robert Wilson's "Einstein On The Beach." The sleeping woman appeared in one of Stock's paintings, *Escape*, 1992.

Stock summed up the advantages he had as a set painter. "Not having a formal background as a designer, and not knowing the limitations of stage design, barriers can be broken when artists work in the theater. We don't know what we can't do. It makes it easier to innovate. I remember a creative meeting for 'The Little Prince' at the Los Angeles Chamber Ballet, which was attended by a visiting choreographer from the Paris Opera Ballet. I presented my sketches and he just said, 'This simply will not work. This is ridiculous.' But Raiford Rogers and I did make it work, and the set proved to be a critical success."

ABOVE: STOCK CONFERS WITH LACB CODIRECTOR, CHOREOGRAPHER AND PRINCIPAL DANCER VICTORIA KOENIG. PHOTO: ERIC YANAGI.

OPPOSITE: STOCK'S SET FOR THE LOS ANGELES CHAMBER BALLET PRODUCTION OF "SO NICE," 1990. PHOTO: ERIC YANAGI.

LEFT: *THE ESCAPE*, 1992. OIL ON CANVAS. 16 X 20 INCHES. PRIVATE COLLECTION.

FOLLOWING PAGES: THE "SLEEPWALK" SET AND DANCERS, 1992. PHOTO: ERIC YANAGI.

LOVE AND MURDER

*"Because the Beautiful is always wonderful, it would be absurd
to suppose that what is wonderful is always beautiful."*
—CHARLES BAUDELAIRE, *THE SALON OF 1859*

Stock's fascination with death inspired
another series the artist calls "The Abyss." Here death, hope, pain, and love
meet at the edge of the void, quite literally on the cliff's edge. In his poem
Delphine et Hippolyte, Charles Baudelaire wrote of the internal abyss: "Opening up
in my being I feel/ A yawning abyss; that abyss is my heart!/ Burning like a
volcano, deep as the void." Stock, too, explored visual metaphors pegged to an
almost morbid preoccupation with angst and heightened feelings.

In *Disenchantment*, 1988, the artist paints a barefoot woman clad only in a thin
summer dress as she stands on a snow-covered cliff. *Ballad*, 1988, frames a man
playing the ukulele at a cliff's edge. In *Relinquishment*, 1989, a dapper figure in a
green overcoat and hat looks down from an alpine cornice as the sky turns a
perfect blue; he stares into the abyss with less fear than curiosity. What if, in his

OPPOSITE: *DRAMAS: THE RETURN TO DARKNESS*, 1993. OIL ON CANVAS. 76 1/4 X 56 1/4 INCHES.

COLLECTION OF THE ARTIST.

ABOVE: *BALLAD*, 1988. OIL ON CANVAS. 64 X 54 1/2 INCHES. COLLECTION OF JOHN AND ROXANNE LANCY.

reverie, he were simply to step off into the void? One might see these figures as postmodern refugees from nineteenth-century Romanticism. Without borrowing obviously, Stock's paintings echo the work of Caspar David Friedrich (1774-1840) (left). There is something strangely comforting in these haunting pictures, as in the retelling of morbid fairytales we heard as children.

In 1987 a San Francisco art dealer, Martin Muller, saw a reproduction of a Stock butler in an art magazine and was struck by its power. Muller recalls, "I was feeling a bit like a depressed butler myself in the love department." That year Stock had his first one-man show at Muller's Modernism Gallery in San Francisco. It was the beginning of an important professional relationship. An intense Swiss intellectual, Muller had a passion for American and Russian avant-garde art, and also for books.

In 1988, this author published *Absinthe: History in a Bottle,* which was the first book to examine the effect that nefarious drink exerted on nineteenth-century French culture. Muller sent Stock a copy of the book. In a whirlwind of excitement, Stock looked at the Impressionist masterpieces such as Édouard Manet's *The Absinthe Drinker,* 1864 (right), and went to work on a new butler. In April of 1988, Muller played host to a black-tie party for one hundred guests at Bix Restaurant to celebrate my book's publication. Real absinthe, bootlegged from Switzerland, was served. Among the guests were Mark Stock, legendary columnist Herb Caen, and artists Mel Ramos and John Register. But by far the biggest star

around corner

wall molding

another room
not particular's
but a dark
shadowy room

THE BUTLER'S IN LOVE

MS '98

ABOVE: DRAWING AND NOTES FOR PAINTINGS IN "THE BUTLER'S IN LOVE" SERIES, 1998.

OPPOSITE: *THE BUTLER'S IN LOVE — ABSINTHE*, 1989. OIL ON CANVAS. 75 1/4 X 64 1/2 INCHES.

COLLECTION OF BIX RESTAURANT, SAN FRANCISCO.

of the evening was a large new Stock painting, *The Butler's In Love — Absinthe*, which was hung above the piano. "I painted it in six days," recalls Stock, "and we hung it wet." It remains the talisman of this popular restaurant and has become Stock's best-known work.

In 1991 Stock left Los Angeles and took a studio in Oakland to be near Modernism Gallery and Oakland-based Magnolia Editions, where he produced a number of prints.

His experience with ballet gave Stock more material for his paintings. He produced a whole series of backstage love dramas that bear comparison to Edgar Degas' paintings of musicians and ballerinas. But where Degas seemed largely concerned with color and the effect of light, Stock focuses on mood conveyed by facial expression and the dramatic gesture. And when the same characters appear in several canvases, one might infer that they are part of an ongoing narrative. In one picture, for example, Stock portrays a balding musician reading a letter with great

intensity, while another canvas offers us an intimate glimpse of the same man confronting a ballerina in a love spat.

In 1992 a new character appeared in the Stock repertoire — a clown in harlequin suit. "I happened to be in a costume shop and saw this great harlequin outfit with the diamond pattern and just had to have it," he said. Far from being giddy, pratfalling hams, Stock's clowns passionately embrace ballerinas back-

ABOVE: MARK STOCK IN A 1988 PHOTO STUDY FOR *RELINQUISHMENT*, 1989.

LEFT: *MARTIN MULLER'S 40TH BIRTHDAY PARTY AT TRADER VIC'S*, 1993. LITHOGRAPH. 8 1/2 X 11 INCHES.

OPPOSITE: *RELINQUISHMENT*, 1989. OIL ON CANVAS. 72 X 52 INCHES. PRIVATE COLLECTION.

OPPOSITE: *MARTIN MULLER AT LA PALETTE, PARIS,* 1990. OIL ON CANVAS. 20 1/2 X 33 INCHES.

COLLECTION OF MARTIN MULLER.

ABOVE LEFT: *BEAUTY IS THE BEGINNING OF TERROR,* 1989. OIL ON CANVAS. 57 X 70 1/2 INCHES.

COURTESY OF MODERNISM GALLERY.

ABOVE RIGHT: *DOUG BIEDERBECK,* 1989. OIL ON CANVAS, 20 X 16 INCHES.

COLLECTION OF DOUG BIEDERBECK.

ABOVE: *MUSICIAN WITH LETTER*, 1987. OIL ON CANVAS. 66 X 55 INCHES. COLLECTION OF THE ARTIST.

PREVIOUS PAGES: MARK STOCK, MODERNISM GALLERY OWNER MARTIN MULLER, BARNABY CONRAD III AND RE-

ALIST PAINTER JOHN REGISTER AT A DINNER PARTY IN SAN FRANCISCO'S BIX RESTAURANT ON APRIL 17, 1989.

MULLER THREW THE PARTY TO CELEBRATE CONRAD'S BIRTHDAY AND THE PUBLICATION OF HIS BOOK *ABSINTHE:*

HISTORY IN A BOTTLE (CHRONICLE BOOKS). ONE OF STOCK'S BEST-KNOWN BUTLER PAINTINGS, *THE BUTLER'S IN LOVE*

— ABSINTHE, 1989, WAS UNVEILED AT THE EVENT AND STILL HANGS ABOVE THE PIANO AT BIX.

THE TRYST, 1988. OIL ON CANVAS. 50 X 63 INCHES. COLLECTION OF BRENDA WOODARD.

PICNIC FOR ONE, 1992. OIL ON CANVAS ON MASONITE. 29 X 34 INCHES.

COLLECTION OF MARGRET JHIN WALSH AND PETER A. WALSH.

OPPOSITE: *TO BE FOREVER REMEMBERED*, 1992. OIL ON CANVAS. 34 X 29 INCHES.

COLLECTION OF STEVE TISCH.

THE LOVERS, 1989. OIL ON CANVAS. 60 X 75 INCHES.

COLLECTION OF ELIZABETH GUTHRIDGE AND DAVID J. MATTHEWS.

THE GUEST, 1989. OIL ON CANVAS. 52 X 73 INCHES. PRIVATE COLLECTION.

stage or become jealous voyeurs peering through parted curtains at their object of desire. "The clown might be seen an extension of Chaplin," observes Stock, "but of course there's a great tradition in European painting, from the clowns of Boucher and Watteau to Picasso's harlequins."

Guy Lampard, an avid collector of Stock's work, told me a story that might apply to Stock's clowns and harlequins. "There was a man who was very despondent who walked into a doctor's office in Essen in the Ruhr Valley in the mid-nineteenth century," Lampard says. "He explained to the German doctor that he was extremely unhappy and depressed with his life, and didn't see much reason to go on living. The doctor tried to convince this man that there were reasons for living and that he should not give up hope. Unfortunately, little seemed to improve the patient's spirits. Near the end of the session, the doctor said the circus was in town, and that Grimaldi the clown would be performing. Grimaldi was known throughout the land as the funniest man in the entire world. He could make everybody laugh and forget their cares. The physician counseled his patient to go to the circus that night, to laugh and forget his cares, if only briefly. As the doctor finished saying this, the man slowly looked up. 'But Doctor, you don't understand,' he said. 'I *am* Grimaldi.'"

Though he had moved to the Bay Area, Stock maintained his fascination with Los Angeles. In 1995 he painted a series inspired by the Hollywood sign that

A SEVENTEENTH CENTURY HARLEQUIN. (BETTMANN/CORBIS)

OPPOSITE: DETAIL OF *HARLEQUIN*, 1993. OIL ON CANVAS. 74 X 55 INCHES. COLLECTION OF THE ARTIST.

ABOVE: *HARLEQUIN HEAD #2*, 1997. OIL ON CANVAS. 36 X 28 INCHES. PRIVATE COLLECTION.

OPPOSITE: DETAIL OF *HARLEQUIN*, 1993. OIL ON CANVAS. 76 X 53 1/4 INCHES.

COLLECTION OF GUY LAMPARD AND SUZANNE BADENHOOP.

ABOVE LEFT: *THE KISS #2*, 1992. OIL ON CANVAS ON MASONITE. 47 3/4 X 40 INCHES.

COLLECTION OF BIX RESTAURANT, SAN FRANCISCO.

ABOVE RIGHT: *THE VIOLINIST*, 1989. OIL ON CANVAS. 58 1/2 X 48 INCHES. PRIVATE COLLECTION.

dominates the hillside above the city. The idea came out of a conversation with actor/director Dale Howard, an old friend (and son of actor John Howard, who starred in *The Philadelphia Story*), who suggested, "Why not paint the sign one letter at a time?" The idea appealed to Stock. There were precedents in Jasper Johns' "Number Series" paintings and prints, and David Hockney's "Alphabet Series" drawings. But at approximately eighty-four by sixty-two inches apiece, Stock's "Hollywood" paintings are more than double the size of the Johns and Hockney masterpieces. Each letter in Stock's "Hollywood" series is really two paintings in one: a giant alphabetical object with a pop-art graphic punch, and an architectural study set in a natural landscape. This is particularly evident with the letter "O" (opposite), where we stand behind the giant letter's scaffold to overlook the glittering city of Los Angeles at night.

Embedded in the encaustic of these enormous letters are ghostly faces of great stars of the past such as Bogart, Monroe and Brando. As critic, curator and art historian John Yau noted in a 1995 catalog for the Modernism exhibition:

THE HOLLYWOOD SIGN IN 1924. (UPI/CORBIS-BETTMANN)

OPPOSITE: STOCK'S "HOLLYWOOD" SERIES. DETAILED CAPTIONS ON PAGE 157.

"Through his use of collage, Stock transforms the letters into tombstones containing the faces of stars who died young, were killed in car accidents, were blackballed, institutionalized, or involved in a ruinous scandal: Fatty Arbuckle, Louise Brooks, Charlie Chaplin, James Dean, Frances Farmer, Jayne Mansfield, Lana Turner, and Rudolph Valentino. They are the direct evidence of the dream gone sour. For all their simmering glow, Stock's letters remind us of the dark side of Hollywood. The city of golden dreams is also a bleak, noir landscape, a place where fate is merciless in its demands."

Murder has always fascinated him, and in 1997 Stock, working with model Stephanie Dean, produced a series called "A Double Life: A Narrative in Noir." These eight canvases follow the same woman in various stages of a domestic murder. We see her peering through window blinds, and then casually smoking a cigarette next to a body rolled up in a Persian carpet. In other images, she is shown shoving a man's shoe into a furnace and digging in a garden at night to bury a box containing, perhaps, a bundle of love letters, or God-knows-what. It is left to the viewer to solve the mystery.

Finally there's a picture of the woman sitting in a chair — now without her wedding ring — while the white gloves of a faceless butler massage her shoulders. The larger-than-life images are painted in golden brown tones that speak as much of Raymond Chandler as of Caravaggio. "They were inspired by all the film noir I used to watch in Los Angeles," says the artist. "I love murder and intrigue." (See screenwriter Mark Hugh Miller's essay on the subject, page 147.)

Stock begins a painting by dressing his friends in costumes, telling them a story, then lighting them carefully and photographing them. "I get to play director, pro-

GEORGES DE LA TOUR, *THE RE-PENTANT MAGDALENE*, MUSÉE DU LOUVRE, PARIS. STOCK'S INSPIRATION FOR HIS CANDLE IMAGES.

ducer, makeup artist, and cinematographer," he says. He'll then make drawings from the photographs, and enlarge them onto a canvas. Stock's paintings may be postmodern riffs on romanticism, but they are not parodies of or even direct references to film.

In 1999 and 2000 Stock painted a series of candles inspired by the seventeenth century French painter Georges de La Tour (1593-1652), famous for creating unique lighting effects. During a monthlong visit to Paris in 1993, Stock visited the Louvre and was mesmerized by La Tour's use of light in paintings such as *The Repentant Magdalene*, c. 1640 (left). "At the center of La Tour's groupings of figures," notes Stock, "there was always a candle that put out such a warm, rich glow. I decided to look closely at the source of light, at the candle itself."

Enlarged twenty times, the melting wax column becomes a sensual, almost sexual symbol that is tempered by the more spiritual glow of the flame radiating from the wick. One could connect these works at least superficially to the candle paintings produced by Gerhard Richter in the 1980s. Stock, however, states that he had never even seen Richter's work until he was well into his own series. "To be honest," says Stock, "I don't look at a lot of other artists' work." In a world given to cynicism, these warm, glowing pictures may strike some as saccharine or sentimental. On the other hand, they are unafraid of stirring an emotional response in the viewer.

When Stock isn't painting, he's drumming for a jazz trio four nights a week at the Cypress Club in San Francisco. He also plays golf competitively, and practices magic tricks. He's highly methodical, extremely punctual. "I paint in the morning, practice golf in the afternoon, paint some more, then drive across the bridge to play jazz at night," he says. Beginning in 1995, for three years Stock played with veteran bassist John Goodman and the late pianist Donald "Tee"

OPPOSITE: *CANDLE (HOMAGE TO GEORGES DE LA TOUR)*, 1999. OIL ON CANVAS.

62 X 52 INCHES. COLLECTION OF RICK AND DANA DIRICKSON.

ABOVE LEFT: *DON STOCK*, 1997. OIL ON CANVAS. 20 X16 INCHES. COLLECTION OF DON AND JUDY STOCK.

ABOVE RIGHT: *THOMAS BERNARD STOCK*, 1997. OIL ON CANVAS. 20 X 16 INCHES.

COLLECTION OF THOMAS BERNARD STOCK.

OPPOSITE: *LANGUISH*. 1998. OIL ON CANVAS. 62 X 52 INCHES. COLLECTION OF

BARRY AND PATTI LEMIEUX.

TOP ROW LEFT TO RIGHT:

ADRIANNA POPE, 1994. OIL ON CANVAS. 32 X 25 1/4 INCHES. COLLECTION OF ADRIANNA POPE.

LILI, 1991. OIL ON CANVAS. 70 1/4 X 57 1/4 INCHES. PRIVATE COLLECTION.

JARED GOSS, 1994. OIL ON CANVAS. 20 X 16 INCHES. COLLECTION OF JARED GOSS.

BOTTOM ROW LEFT TO RIGHT:

KENT LOGAN, 1997. OIL ON CANVAS. 20 X 16 INCHES. COLLECTION OF VICKI AND KENT LOGAN.

FABIO MASSIMO FAGGI, 2000. OIL ON CANVAS. 20 X 16 INCHES. COLLECTION OF FABIO MASSIMO FAGGI.

VICKI LOGAN, 1997. OIL ON CANVAS. 20 X 16 INCHES. COLLECTION OF VICKI AD KENT LOGAN.

TOP ROW LEFT TO RIGHT:

ALAIN BORER, 1994. OIL ON CANVAS. 20 X 16 INCHES. COLLECTION OF ALAIN BORER.

PIERRE PRENTKI, 1995. OIL ON CANVAS. 20 X 16 INCHES. COLLECTION OF MARK MULLER.

PROUST REMEMBERED, 1997. OIL ON CANVAS. 20 X 16 INCHES. PRIVATE COLLECTION.

BOTTOM ROW LEFT TO RIGHT:

LUIGI, 1993. OIL ON CANVAS. 17 3/8 X 14 1/4 INCHES. COLLECTION OF LUIGI MARATEO.

AUDREY LEE, 1988. OIL ON CANVAS. 18 1/4 X 15 1/4 INCHES. PRIVATE COLLECTION.

MARK MILLER, 2000. OIL ON CANVAS. 20 X 16 INCHES. COLLECTION OF THE ARTIST.

Evgeni Voronin, 2000. Oil on canvas. 72 x 60 inches. Collection of the artist. Stock was inspired by the persona of the grand comedic magician Voronin, a central figure at the dinner circus Teatro Zinzanni.

TOP LEFT : *ILONA MIKO*, 2000. OIL ON CANVAS. 16 X 20 INCHES. COLLECTION OF ILONA MIKO.

TOP RIGHT: *ROXANNE CANEPA*, 2000. OIL ON CANVAS. 20 X 16 INCHES. COLLECTION OF ROXANNE CANEPA.

BOTTOM LEFT: *OLIVIER WEBER-CAFLISCH*, 1999. OIL ON CANVAS. 20 X 16 INCHES. PRIVATE COLLECTION.

BOTTOM RIGHT: *DIANE VON FURSTENBERG*, 1993. OIL ON CANVAS. 24 X 18 INCHES. PRIVATE COLLECTION.

Carson, who had toured for three years with Ella Fitzgerald and then performed with the Count Basie Orchestra for nine. (As his health failed, Basie handpicked Carson to replace him as pianist.) "It was a privilege to play with Tee and John," says Stock. "Every night we played together I learned something new. Tremendous artists and friends." Stock had the honor of recording with Carson on his 1998 CD, *Tee Carson and Friends*. Stock has also set the beat for notable pianists Rob Schneiderman, Frank Jackson, Alan Steger, Gary Rowe, Shanna Carlson, and the late Merrill Hoover and Flip Nuñez.

Stock's passion for golf is not at odds with painting, and he continues to compete in local tournaments in the Bay Area. Fellow painter and golf partner Christopher Brown commented, "Mark's got the most versatile pair of hands." What is the appeal of golf to an artist? "It's a quiet game," says Brown. "Walking a course is like playing through a site-specific sculpture. You're constantly aware of distances and proportions. It's the same with painting."

A CASUAL CONVERSATION BE-TWEEN STOCK AND PIANIST TEE CARSON LED TO STOCK'S REGULAR PERFOR-MANCES WITH THE JOHN GOODMAN TRIO AT SAN FRANCISCO'S CYPRESS CLUB. PHOTO: JOHN MCNALLY, 1995.

FAR LEFT: DETAIL OF *DONALD (TEE) CARSON*, 1996. OIL ON CANVAS. 36 X 26 INCHES. COLLECTION OF ROBIN CARSON.

LEFT: DETAIL OF *JOHN GOODMAN AND FRIEND*, 1996. OIL ON CANVAS. 18 X 24 INCHES. COLLECTION OF JOHN AND DEE GOODMAN.

OPPOSITE: *HOMAGE TO GEORGES DE LA TOUR #3*, 2000. OIL ON CANVAS. 72 X 60 INCHES.
COURTESY OF MODERNISM GALLERY.

A SCENE FROM "TEE TO GREEN," MARK STOCK'S 1979 PERFORMANCE PIECE FEATURING, LEFT TO
RIGHT, NANCY REESE, DALE HOWARD AND STOCK. PHOTO: KEITH ELLIOT.

DEAD GOLFER. 1992. OIL ON CANVAS ON MASONITE. 31 1/2 X 48 INCHES.

COLLECTION OF JEFFRY WEISMAN.

As if to reinforce this contention, Stock hands me a clipping that quotes New York painter Chuck Close on the sport: "Golf is the only sport in which you move from the general to the specific, in an ideal number of discrete moves. Each move is a correction. The first stroke is kind of a leap of faith that the hole is out there. The second stroke corrects that, and the third corrects that, and by then, hopefully, you're on the green. And with any luck, at a par-four hole, you can place that ball in a four-and-a-quarter-inch-diameter circle … What you did is find it in the landscape. You found the hole."

In Stock's grandest work, he has not only found the hole in the landscape, he has enlarged it to the size of a billboard. In 1999 Stock, working with consultant Merry Norris, won a commission to create a series of sixty-one-by-thirty-five-foot outdoor murals for a film production company, Los Angeles Center Studios, a complex of sound stages located at Fifth and Beaudry. From several blocks away one sees two mysterious images — like those of a split-screen cinema — looming from adjacent buildings. The panel on the right depicts a woman pressing a glass up to a wall to hear what's happening in the room next door. The panel on the left shows a giant vase of flowers smashing on impact. What do these pictures mean? After their unveiling, Stock mentioned the influence of Roman Polanski's *The Tenant* and David Lynch's *Blue Velvet*. But beyond that, he offered few clues.

"It's the slowest movie in town," Stock said, referring to the fact that only two panels would be unveiled annually over a three-year period. "You'll just have to wait for the next installment. I've been sworn to secrecy. Like a good butler, I can't tell you what happens — not yet."

Even if the butler *did* do it.

OPPOSITE: *BUMP*, 1999 (DETAIL). OIL ON CANVAS. 52 X 62 INCHES. COLLECTION OF BARNABY CONRAD III.

FOLLOWING PAGES: *IN RAPTURE: SCENE 1*, AN OUTDOOR MURAL SERIES FOR THE

LOS ANGELES CENTER STUDIOS. PHOTO: RICK MEYER, *LOS ANGELES TIMES*.

POINT OF NO RETURN:
MARK STOCK AND FILM NOIR

BY MARK HUGH MILLER

I n most dramatic films, there is a moment early on where a key character crosses a line. He (or she) does something that cannot be undone, after which a return to the other side is impossible. A promise is given. A lie is told. A secret is discovered, a criminal plot hatched. Nothing can ever be the same again.

Screenwriters call these moments "plot points," and no film genre relies more heavily on them than film noir — a term coined in 1946 by French critic Nino Frank to describe a style of American films made between the Depression and the McCarthy era of the mid-1950s. Film noir — literally "black film"— referred not to these movies' shadowy black-and-white images but rather their gloomy existentialist sentiments. In film noir, bad things happen for no good reason, the innocent suffer, and love seldom conquers anything at all. Good

Untitled ("A Double Life" #8), 1998. Oil on canvas. 62 x 52 inches. Collection of Dennis and Kathleen Abbe.

rarely triumphs over evil, and, regardless of the outcome, the world is indifferent to it, and unchanged.

In much of his work, Mark Stock is a painterly *cinéaste* of noir. Working on canvas in vivid color, Stock takes a narrative approach and makes consistent use of certain characters and emotions. The quintessential noir characters are the hard-boiled detective and the seductive femme fatale. Stock's equivalents include his lonely man on the precipice (like the archetypal noir detective, he often wears a fedora and overcoat), the clown (as with noir males, he conceals his sadness behind a professional mask), and his tormented butler (trapped in a costume of discretion). Like film noir females, Stock's women are hard to read — their expressions are often ambiguous, their emotions open to speculation.

What sets film noir apart from other genres is the unity of its world view. In noir, as in Stock's work, narrative patterns and character emotions recur over and over — evil is at work, love is betrayed, secrets are whispered, kisses are stolen. At the end of the day, loneliness and despair arrive with the twilight. In noir, the emotions propelling the main characters are alienation and obsession. The latter usually surfaces as blind love, cold-blooded greed, a thirst for revenge, or selfless concern for a friend's well-being. The archetypal noir male lives without benefit of social connections. He is usually a disillusioned romantic, a character evident in much of Stock's work. Like a private eye — or a butler — he is privy to society's secrets but is not part of society. He is a well-dressed outsider.

Although noir women usually stand higher on the social and economic lad-

OPPOSITE: *Synchronize*, 1997. Oil on canvas. 62 x 52 inches. Collection of Paul and Cindy Levy.

Untitled ("A Double Life" #6), 1997. Oil on canvas. 42 x 52 inches.

Courtesy of Modernism Gallery.

ders than the male protagonist — they are the ones served by butlers — they too tend to be outsiders. Often they are only outsiders posing as insiders. They are hiding unpleasant pasts behind reinvented personas. A noir female may fall in love, but her overriding emotion will always be self-interest.

Stock's images are replete with romance, ardor, anguish, deception, loneliness, yearning, disappointment, and betrayal. They resemble moments depicted on storyboards — panels created for directors, in advance of filming, that depict key camera setups for every scene. (In the golden years of Hollywood's studio era, many storyboard artists were classically schooled painters.) Stock's tormented butler is a quintessentially noir character. When he gazes at the empty wine glass bearing the red imprint of a woman's rouged lips, his obsession with an impossible intimacy shreds his emotions. Anguished over his powerlessness in the world — a psychological trademark of noir — he slumps against a wall. Like the noir detective, he is not the social equal of the people who employ him; he may present the object of his desire with a flute of champagne, but to speak to her is forbidden. His torment is so unbearable that he retreats, as he does in *The Butler's in Love #37*, 1987. The white-gloved servant leans against a solid wall symbolizing the barrier separating them.

Despite his despair, his professionalism prevails, and he maintains his crisp formality.

Stock is hardly the first narrative artist to create images that appear cinematic. Cindy

IRENE MANNING AND HUMPHREY BOGART IN *THE BIG SHOT*, RELEASED IN 1942. (CORBIS)

Sherman's fictional photographic self-portraits, for example, mimic stills from films and paparazzi tabloid shots of disconcerted stars. Stock's intent, however, is not to reinterpret cinema, or burlesque its conventions. His images flow instead from a personal view of the world that is essentially noir. Like a director of silent film, he chooses visual moments that make clear not only what has happened, or is about to happen, but also suggest likely consequences. Other images — reflections in mirrors, a close-up of a face illumined by a candle — recall German expressionist films, an antecedent of noir. A viewer familiar with Stock's work, like a moviegoer conversant in the conventions of noir, can often extrapolate the broad outlines of the story behind a single image.

In the untitled fifth painting in Stock's 1997 series "A Double Life" (opposite), a woman reaches into a Chinese vase. Is she hiding something — or retrieving it? Is she acting for good or evil? In #2 of the series, she sits on the floor and calmly smokes a cigarette. Beside her, a man's feet poke from the end of a rolled-up Persian carpet.

But will she keep her secret? Not if the window through which the young dinner-jacketed voyeur in *The Viewer*, 1991, is hers. The voyeur, however, does not appear disturbed, merely curious. On his tiptoes, perhaps he sees only her and does not notice the dead man at her feet. His stance — hands folded behind his back — suggests a self-conscious pose of innocence as insurance against discovery. (He should not be there.) He is in any case an outsider. As for what else he is, we are left to speculate. In a noir film, this could be a plot point: from here on, her scheme will begin to unravel; her doom is foretold. Pure noir.

CHRONOLOGY

Born Frankfurt, Germany, 1951

EDUCATION

St. Petersburg Junior College, St. Petersburg, FL, AA, 1972
University of South Florida, Tampa, BA, 1976

ONE-PERSON EXHIBITIONS

2001 Modernism, San Francisco

1999 Armory Art Center, West Palm Beach

Suggested Evidence; New Paintings, Modernism, San Francisco

1997 *A Double Life*, Modernism, San Francisco

1996 *Mark Stock; Paintings and Designs 1986-1996*, University of South Florida, Tampa

1995 *Hollywood*, Modernism, San Francisco (catalogue)

1994 Modernism, San Francisco

1992 *Stage & Costume Designs for the Theater & Other Works on Paper 1977-1992*, Modernism, San Francisco

New Paintings, Modernism, San Francisco

1991 Susan Johnson Gallery, Tampa

1990 Modernism, San Francisco

1989 Modernism, San Francisco

J. Rosenthal Fine Arts, Chicago

1988 Modernism, San Francisco

Tortue Gallery, Santa Monica

1987 Modernism, San Francisco

Tortue Gallery, Santa Monica

1986 *Mark Stock, California Contemporary Artist 32*, Laguna Art Museum, Laguna Beach

1985 Tortue Gallery, Santa Monica

1981 Hirschl & Adler Modern, New York

1980 University of South Florida, Tampa

GROUP EXHIBITIONS

1999 *Contemporary American Realist Drawings*, The Art Institute of Chicago

Inside Stories, Armory Art Center, West Palm Beach, Florida

20th Anniversary Exhibition, Part I, Modernism

Drawings from the Jalane & Richard Davidson Collection, The Art Institute of Chicago

1998 *Selected Works: Jean-Charles BLAIS; R. CRUMB; Sheldon GREENBERG; Gottfried HELNWEIN; Gus HEINZE; Mark STOCK; Jerry KEARNS; Naomie KREMER; Curtis RIPLEY*, Modernism, San Francisco

1997 *Paintings & Works on Paper: Jean-Michel BASQUIAT; Gus HEINZE; Gottfried HELNWEIN; Jerry KEARNS; Mel RAMOS; John REGISTER, Arsen ROJE; Mark STOCK; Roland TOPOR; Andy WARHOL*, Modernism, San Francisco

Donald Farnsworth, Mark Stock, Judith Litvich Contemporary Arts at Idea House, San Francisco

1996 *The Cigar*, Modernism, San Francisco

Dan McCleary; John Nava; Mark Stock, Magnolia Editions, San Francisco

1995 *Martini Culture*, Modernism, San Francisco

1993 *Love and Other Attractions*, Contemporary Arts Forum, Santa Barbara

1991 *Handcolored Prints from the Achenbach Foundation for Graphic Art*, Palace of the Legion of Honor, San Francisco

For Better or For Worse: Artist's Views on Romance, Monterey Peninsula Museum of Art

The Palm Tree Show, Modernism, San Francisco

Aspects of Figural Painting in Southern California, Tatistcheff Gallery, Santa Monica

1990 *Contra Costa Collects*, Bedford Gallery, Walnut Creek, California

Surface Printing in the 1980's, Jane Voorhees Zimmerli Art Museum, Rutgers University, New Jersey

1989 *Configurations*, Security Pacific Plaza, Los Angeles

1987 *Figuration/Imagination*, California State University, San Bernardino

1986 *California in New York*, Tatistcheff Gallery, New York

1985 *Newcomers '85*, Municipal Art Gallery, Los Angeles

1984 *The American Artist as Printmaker*, Brooklyn Museum of Art

1983 *Gene Baro Collects*, Brooklyn Museum of Art

Recent Acquisitions of Fine Prints, Thomas Jefferson Building of the Library of Congress, Washington, DC

1980-81 *American Drawings in Black and White, 1970-80*, Brooklyn Museum of Art

1980 *Drawings to Benefit the Foundation for Contemporary Performing Arts*, Leo Castelli Gallery, New York

1978-81 *100 New Acquisitions*, Brooklyn Museum of Art

1976 *30 Years of American Printmaking*, Brooklyn Museum of Art

COLLABORATIONS/COMMISSIONS

1999-2001 *"Enrapture,"* six murals, Los Angeles Center Studio

1992 Set design, Los Angeles Chamber Ballet production of "Sleepwalk," premiered Japan America Theatre, Los Angeles

Set design, Ballet Pacifica production of "Personal Statements — Common Knowledge," choreographed by Tina Gerstler, premiered University of California, Irvine

1990 Set design, Los Angeles Chamber Ballet production of "So Nice," premiered Japan America Theatre, Los Angeles

1989 Set design, Los Angeles Chamber Ballet production of "Dmitri," premiered Japan America Theatre, Los Angeles

1988 Set and costume design, Los Angeles Chamber Ballet production of "Orpheus; A Ballet-Opera in One Act," premiered Japan America Theatre, Los Angeles

1986 Set and costume design, Los Angeles Chamber Ballet production of "The Little Prince," premiered Japan America Theatre, Los Angeles

1984 Set design, playwright Nancy Barr's "Johnny Dakota Writes It Down," premiered Night House Theatre, Los Angeles

1981 Set design, Rudy Perez Dance Company production of "Tracers" and "Take Stock," premiered Royce Hall, University of California, Los Angeles

GIRLS, GIRLS, GIRLS. 1994. OIL ON CANVAS. 50 1/4 X 60 INCHES. COURTESY OF MODERNISM GALLERY.

PUBLIC COLLECTIONS

Achenbach Foundation for Graphic Art, San Francisco

Brooklyn Museum of Art

De Saisset Museum, Santa Clara, California

Library of Congress, Washington, D.C.

Museum of Modern Art, New York

National Gallery of Art, Washington, D.C.

San Francisco Museum of Modern Art

Speed Museum, Louisville

Tampa Museum, Tampa

University of South Florida, Tampa

Jane Voorhees Zimmerli Art Museum, Rutgers, New Jersey

AWARDS

Distinguished Alumnus Achievement Award, University of South
    Florida, Tampa, 1993

ABYSS, 1989. OIL ON CANVAS. 75 X 57 INCHES. PRIVATE COLLECTION.

BIBLIOGRAPHY

Nob Hill Gazette, Aug 1999 (illus).

Sasha Anawalt. Ballet Review, Summer 1990.

——. "Arabesques a la Woody Allen?" *NY Times*, Arts and Leisure, Feb
    12, 1989, pp. 8 & 23.

——. "The Legend of 'Orpheus' is Reborn," *L.A. Herald Examiner*, Feb
    26, 1988, Dance, p. 33.

——. "L.A. Ballet Gives Life to 'Little Prince'," *L.A. Herald Examiner*, Jan
    31, 1986, p. 34.

——. *L.A. Herald Examiner*, Feb 3, 1986.

Shelley Baumsten. "Doing 'Dimitri' for Kicks," *L.A. Times*, Calendar, Feb
    12, 1989.

——. "L.A. Chamber Ballet Tackles 'Orpheus'," *L.A. Times*, Calendar, Feb
    14, 1988.

Martin Bernheimer. *L.A. Times*, Feb 3, 1986.

——. "Rudy Perez & Co. at Royal Hall," *L.A. Times*, Calendar, Jan 19,
    1981.

Jeanie Blake. *The Times Picayune*, New Orleans, Apr 19, 1976.

Jan Breslauer. *L.A. Weekly*, Feb 17, 1989.

Doug Buehl. "Modern modern," *Oracle* (University of San Francisco),
    Mar 6, 1996.

California Magazine, Dec 1987 (illus).

Mindy Cameron. "On the Cover," *Nob Hill Gazette*, Vol. 17, No. 9, Sep
    1995 (color illus).

Alberta Collier. *The Times Picayune*, New Orleans, Apr 5, 1976.

Llewellyn Crain. "Prince Reigns Strong," *Daily News*, L.A. Life, Feb 3,
    1986, p. 19.

Jeanette Crane. *St. Petersburg Times*, Jul 22, 1971.

Martin A. David. "Prince Charming," *L.A. Weekly*, Vol. 8, No. 10, Jan 31-
    Feb 6, 1986.

——. "Dance Spectrum," *Drama-Logue*, Feb 13-19, 1986.

Joie Davidow. "Two by Nancy Barr," *L.A. Weekly*, Aug 24-30, 1984.

Lucia Dewey. "Dance Spectrum," *Drama-Logue*, Mar 10-16, 1988.

Holly Finn. "Brushes with Magic," *Financial Times*, Aug 7-8, 1999.

Michael Gilda. "Art," *L.A. Weekly*, May 8-14, 1987, p. 43 (b/w illus).

Susan Geer. "A Dramatic Exhibition is Staged at Laguna Beach Art Mu-
    seum," *Orange County Register*, Feb 14, 1986.

Don Gray. "Mark Stock, Nancy Reese, Dan McCleary," *Artnews*, Vol 86,
    No. 5, May 1987, p. 164 (illus).

Gerald Haggerty. *Figuration/Imagination; Paintings by Dan McCleary, Hank
    Pitcher, Mark Stock*, University Art Gallery, California State Univer-
    sity, San Bernardino (exhibition catalogue), 1987.

T. Hansen, D. Mickenberg, J. Moser & B. Walker. *Printmaking in America,
    Collaborative Prints and Presses 1960-1990* (illus p. 36, 57, 123 &
    214).

Diane Heilenman. "Speed Exhibit of Works by 28 Artists Shows There
    is No California Look," *Courier-Journal*, Louisville, Kentucky, May
    11, 1986, P. 110 (b/w illus).

Michelle Huneven. "The Butler's in Love," *California Magazine*, May 1988,
    p. 114 (color illus).

Hilton Kramer. "American Drawings of the '70s at Brooklyn," *NY Times*, Weekend, Nov 28, 1980, pp. C1 & C18

Marina La Palma. *Artweek*, Sep 9, 1989.

Jody Leader. "Chamber Ballet Blooms in a Rugged Dance Scene," *Daily News*, L.A. Life, Feb 26, 1988.

——. "L.A. Chamber Dancers Take 'Dmitri' and Run," *Daily News*, L.A. Life, Feb 18, 1989, p. 16.

——. "Ballet Goes Bananas in 'Dmitri'," *Daily News*, L.A. Life, Feb 15, 1989, p. 13.

Roberta Loach. *Visual Dialog*, Fall 1976.

Kathryn Maese. "L.A. Center Studios' Art Project Creates a Downtown Curio," *Los Angeles Downtown News*, Mar 20, 2000, pp. 1, 6.

Mary Ann Marger. "Images of Society," *Tampa Tribune*, Apr 12. 1996, p. 25 (color illus.).

Robert Martin. *Tampa Times*, Jun 23, 1980.

——. *Tampa Times*, Jan 21, 1975.

Joanne Milani. "Photos and movies leave mark on paintings of USF graduate," *Tampa Tribune*, Apr 12, 1996, Bay Life, pp. 1 & 9 (color & b/w illus.).

——. "Art," *Tampa Tribune*, Friday Extra, Best Bets, Apr 12, 1996, p. 3 (color illus.).

Suzanne Muchnic. "A Story, but No Writing, Is on the Wall," *Los Angeles Times*, Sunday Calendar, Jan 2, 2000.

——. "Galleries/Santa Monica," *L.A. Times*, Part VI, May 1, 1987 (b/w illus.).

——. "Galleries/Santa Monica," *L.A. Times*, Dec 6, 1985 (illus.).

Kristine McKenna, "Post-Modernism at Security Pacific," *L.A. Times*, Calendar, Part IV, Aug 22, 1989, pp. 7 & 9.

——. "Laguna Museum Shows Stock, McMillen Works," *L.A. Times*, Calendar, Feb 11, 1986, pp. 1 & 7.

Helen Peppard. "Chamber Ballet Gives Prince of a Show," *Daily News*, Feb 23, 1987.

——. *Variety*, Feb 6, 1989.

Donna Perlmutter. "National Reviews," *Dance Magazine*, Jun, 1989.

——. "When You Play it Safe, Don't Expect Excitement," *L.A. Herald Examiner*, Oct 5, 1983, p. 33.

——. *L.A. Times*, Jan 19, 1981.

Pierre Picot. "Seductive Hopes and Dreams," *Artweek*, Vol. 19, No. 37, Nov 5, 1988, p. 3 (b/w illus.).

David Robinson. *Chaplin: His Life and Art*, Collins, 1985.

Lynn Rothman. "L.A. Story; One Picture Is Worth a Thousand Movies," *University of South Florida*, Summer 1996, pp. 22-23.

Betty Rubinstein. *Tallahassee Democrat*, Dec 21, 1980.

Doug Sadownick. "Pick of the Week," *L.A. Weekly*, Feb 26-Mar 3, 1988.

San Francisco Focus, Dec 1987 (2 b/w illus.).

The Security Pacific Collection; Twenty Years 1970-1990: Prints, Los Angeles, 1990, p. 46 (color illus.).

Louis Segal. "L.A. Chamber Ballet Stages Woody Allen's 'Dmitri'," *L.A. Times*, Calendar, Part V, Feb 18, 1989, p. 12.

——. "New 'Orpheus' in Central L.A.," *L.A. Times*, Calendar, Feb 29, 1988, p. 1-2.

——. *L.A. Times*, Jan 31, 1986.

Betty Shimabukuro. "Common Man Comes Alive; AA Exhibit Focuses on Humanity in Painted Figures," *The Sun*, Living, Oct 10, 1987 (b/w illus).

Don Shirley. "Two by Barr: Artful, Translucent," *L.A. Times*, Aug 17, 1984.

——. "Ballet Review (L.A. Chamber Ballet, The Little Prince)," *L.A. Herald Examiner*, Feb 3, 1986, B5.

Susannah Temko. "Local Galleries Contribute to International Art Fair," *Evening Outlook*, Art, Dec 5, 1986 (illus.).

Linda Tomko. *L.A. Times*, Sep 9, 1980.

Amei Wallach. "The Contemporary Collector's Art," *New York Times Magazine*, Oct 26, 1997, p. 77 (illus).

Ruth Weisburg. "Configurations," *Security Pacific at the Plaza* (catalogue), Jul 1998.

William Wilson. "Galleries/Santa Monica," *L.A. Times*, Oct 12, 1988, Part VI, p. 21.

——. "Newcomer's Show: Good Yet Gauche," *L.A. Times*, Art Review, Part VI, Oct 10, 1985, pp. 2 & 8 (b/w illus).

John Yau. *Mark Stock; Hollywood*, Modernism, San Francisco, 1995.

Elizabeth Zimmer. "'Dmitri' Left Audience Wanting More," *L.A. Herald Examiner*, Feb 18, 1989.

——. "Chamber Ballet Borrows Woody Allen's 'Dmitri'," *L.A. Herald Examiner*, Feb 16, 1989.

Details from the following "Hollywood" series paintings appear on page 125:

Letter H, 1995. Oil, collage and encaustic on linen. 84 x 66 inches. Collection of Lisa and Peter Westley.

Letter O, 1995. Oil, collage and encaustic on linen. 84 x 66 inches. Private collection.

Letter L, 1995. Oil, collage and encaustic on linen. 84 x 47 inches. Collection of Howard and Carol Berl.

Letter L, 1995. Oil, collage and encaustic on linen. 84 x 56 inches. Courtesy of Modernism Gallery.

Letter Y, 1995. Oil, collage and encaustic on linen. 84 x 60 inches. Collection of Steven and Kimberly Schow.

Letter W, 1995. Oil, collage and encaustic on linen. 84 x 47 1/2 inches. Courtesy of Modernism Gallery.

Letter O, 1995. Oil, collage and encaustic on linen. 84 x 51 inches. Collection of Robert and Ellen Little.

Letter O, 1995. Oil, collage, and encaustic on linen. 84 x 62 1/4 inches. Collection of Steve Wilson and Laura Lee Brown.

Letter D, 1995. Oil, collage and encaustic on linen. 84 x 62 1/4 inches. Collection of Boston Consulting Group Inc.

CANDLE INSTALLATION IN MARK STOCK'S OAKLAND STUDIO, WINTER, 1999.

ACKNOWLEDGMENTS

This book would not have been possible without the assistance of Modernism Gallery director Katya Kashkooli, Modernism owner Martin Muller, book designer Tom Morgan, editor Richard Defendorf, and Woodford Press publishers David Burgin and Dan Ross.

Mark Stock, the author and the publishers thank *The Remains of the Day* author Kazuo Ishiguro for his beautifully expressed observations about Mr. Stock's work. Thanks as well to Philip Cohen Photographic and photographer Brian Forrest for documenting Mr. Stock's work with meticulous care.

Mr. Stock also would like to thank the people who have mod- eled for images in this book. They include: Tony Abatemarco, Perla Batalla, Doug Biederbeck, Alain Borer, Roxanne Canepa, Roberto Cromeyer, Barnaby Conrad III, Stephanie Dean, John Goodman, Jared Goss, Susan Falcon Hargraves, Dale and Teda Howard, Andrew Hyman, Brad Johnson, Audrey Lee, James Kelly, Vicki and Kent Logan, Michael Lovelady, Ilona Miko, Mark H. Miller, Lili Monell, Martin Muller, Jan Munroe, Elizabeth Parra, Charlotte Richards, Melinda Ring, Maila Rosa, Ray Seay, Thomas Bernard Stock, Don Stock, John and Sarah Uyeyama, Bil Volker, Diane von Furstenberg, Evgeni Voronin and Olivier Weber-Caflisch.

INDEX

FOLLOWING PAGE: *HOMAGE TO GEORGES DE LA TOUR*, 2000. OIL ON CANVAS.

30 X 24 INCHES. COURTESY OF MODERNISM GALLERY.

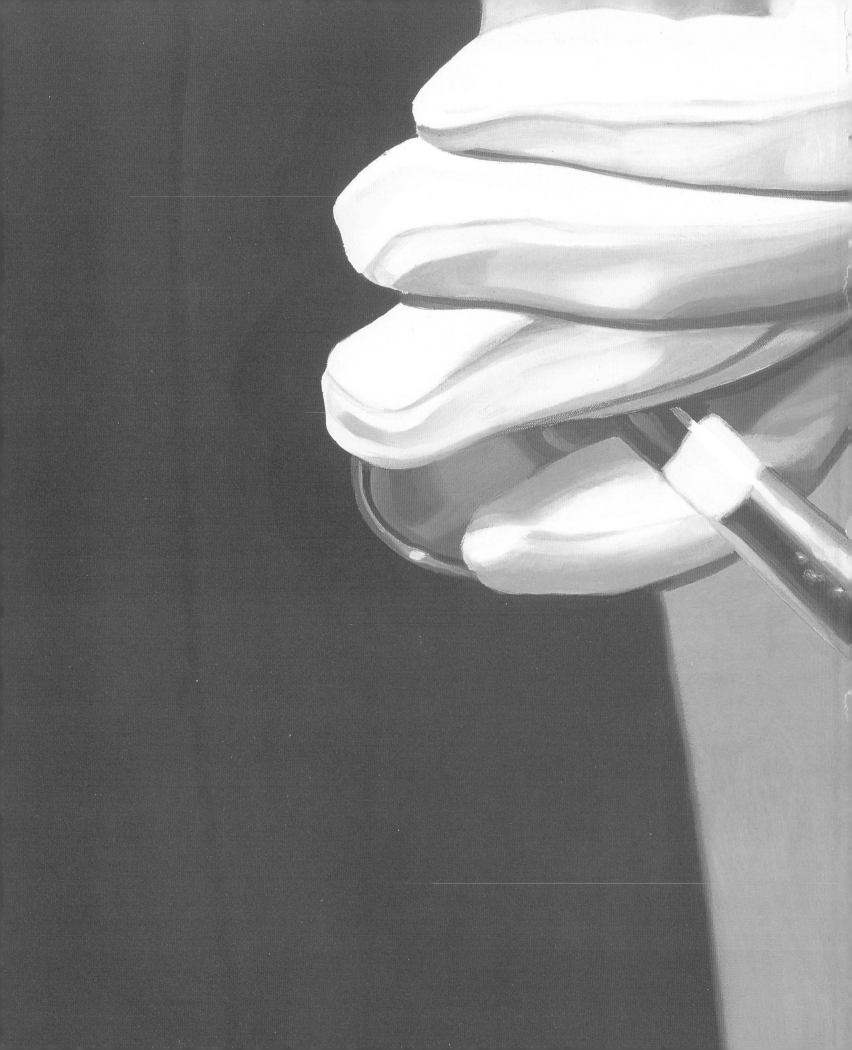